AN

UNCONVENTIONAL

LIFE

AN

UNCONVENTIONAL

LIFE

Where Messes and Magic Collide

By Stacey Robbins

There are people who come into your world and turn it upside down and inside out. They call you on your sh*t and kiss your boo-boos, until you feel so distracted by the love that the pain starts to go away.

Those people are my three amazing guys -- and this book is dedicated to you:

Rock, Caleb, and Seth

*Thank you for healing my soul in places I didn't even know I needed it
And thank you for bringing that healing to the world.*

Table of Contents

Gratitudes

There are the usual cast of suspects of amazing friends who love me through life:

Ken and Lynette Tamplin, David Trotter, Angela Ippolito, Dave Cottam, Mary Alvarado, Laurie and Ralph Umbriaco, August and Hal Brice, Irene and Kent Dunlap, Beth and Michael Prizer, Tracy Panzarella, Susannah Parrish, Carissa Boles, Silvana Balsimelli, Nigel Skeet, Lance and Lyndia Leonard, and Linda Masterson.

A girl would be absolutely giddy to have just one of you in her midst. To have all of you makes me feel exactly what I am: Tremendously rich in friendship and love. Thank you!

I'm grateful for the amazing support of the *Girlfriends Guide to Hashimoto's* team who cheered me on and those who stepped in to read and edit: Lindsey Donhauser, Karen Giacalone, and Courtney Meehan -- as well as my virtual support team of Mikelle Hebeka, Anne-Maree Moore, and Jessi and Stephen Bass who help bring what I do, to life.

Special extra Thank You's to:

David Trotter for walking the daily path of life with me -- in friendship, business, spirituality, and creativity, and for being the kind of friend who can introduce this book to the world on my behalf.

Irene Dunlap, good Lord, woman, we've done a LOT of life together the last 20 years! Thank you for bringing all that *Chicken Soup* experience and your big heart and belief to the editing process. You rock!

Josh Reeves for being the unicorn of playful, honest, authentic spirituality. It's nice to know that people like you are in the world. How honored am I to call you a new and treasured friend.

And saving the best for last...

I'm especially grateful for this man who has not only endured, but savored my particular brand of crazy for nearly 30 years: Rock, thank you for loving me inside and out, through emotional, financial, and physical "thick and thin," -- through bitchy and kind, through book-writing and not book-writing (which is pretty much the same as bitchy and kind). I love you, sweetheart. Thanks for riding the Not-Boring Rollercoaster by my side.

Please make sure your seatbelt is fastened and that the handle bars are securely in place -- we have many more rides to go.

And our two brave children: Caleb and Seth -- you chose an Unconventional Mom and Dad and signed up for living an Unconventional Life -- probably because you are Unconventional Souls. Thank you for being adventurous, in the just right kind of ways that allow us to do off-the-beaten track kind of living. And thank you for being settled and stable enough, internally, to know where your True North is, no matter where we are and what we do. I learn from you constantly and I'm eternally grateful to be your mom and for you to be my sons and my teachers. I love you both, "forever and heaven."

Foreword

I don't remember meeting Stacey Robbins...*ever*.

There *was* that time in 2008 when my family and I were walking up to a fall festival at a church as Stacey and her family were pulling away. She stopped the car and warmly greeted my wife as if they knew each other. It turns out that Stacey had been cheering us on from a distance as we were recovering from a major marital tailspin.

And, then...*poof!*
She was in my life.

That's how she works. You don't remember *when* she comes into your life, but you just know that your life is different because of her presence.

Bump into her at the farmer's market?
There she is with a radiant smile - welcoming all who come along her path.

Struggling with a health condition?
Her research is extensive, and she generously shares with those in need.

Trying to make a relationship work?
Her insight and fresh perspective allow hearts to reconnect.

Wrestling with meaning, spirituality, or faith?
Her journey is an open book, and her wisdom flows from a source called Love.

Dreaming about exploring the world with your family?
Her ability to dream adventures into fruition has propelled her family around the globe.

What does all this add up to?
Stacey lives an unconventional life that inspires people to dream what's possible - rather than settle for what's probable.

As I've wrestled with my faith, my marriage, and the direction of my work as a filmmaker, she always asks, "What's possible?"

Yes, we know what's probable. The status quo, the norm, and whatever our culture is willing to accept.

BUT...what is possible? *"If you could dream about your health or relationship or finances or spirituality, what would you long to experience?"* She has asked me some variation of this question with both her words and her life.

Stacey doesn't settle for what's probable. Instead, she challenges me (and you) to open our minds and hearts to options we might not otherwise consider. It's not an in-your-face kind of challenge. She's more like a 'loving tour guide for the soul' who shows up just when you need her and hands out compasses and binoculars and water and organic snacks. She seems to have run out of one-way maps years ago, but she *is* more than willing to share her wisdom about the paths she has travelled and the paths she has learned about from others.

It's up to you what you do with the wisdom.
She doesn't get all judgy about what path you take.

(Case in point. While we talk on the phone, she's usually munching on gluten-free, wheat-free, taste-free chips while rubbing an ancient health potion all over herself right before starting yoga. Meanwhile,

I'm microwaving a leftover burrito covered in cheese as I gulp down a Diet Dr. Pepper.)

She genuinely believes we all find different paths toward health, wholeness, and fulfillment - in our own timing. Her focus is on Love, and that's how she makes me feel...*loved.*

In our friendship (and through this book), she creates space for me to know that I am loved just the way I am. I'm not loved *if* I say or do the right thing. I'm loved right now in the midst of me trying to love my wife, invest in my kids, live out my own dreams, and eat that yummy carb-loaded burrito.

In our friendship (and in this book), she is incredibly generous with her knowledge, wisdom, and heart. If she knows something, she'll share it without expectation that I'll implement it in my life. If she has experienced something, she'll offer it as one perspective on life. And, if she senses something below the surface, she's willing to ask the tough questions and create moments of vulnerability if I'm open to it.

She will do the same for you thing through the stories and insights in this book. The words are personal – from Stacey to you. If it were possible, she would share each of these stories with you face to face – heart to heart. That's the type of person she is. So...please know...this book is a gift of stories and insights from the heart of Stacey Robbins – filled with love as she asks you the question, "What's possible in your life?"

David Trotter
Filmmaker

INTRODUCTION:
A Magical, Healing Adventure

So, what do you do when...

Your 12 year-old pulls himself out of school in the middle of the year because of a bullying issue...

Your husband comes home and announces his division is sold and that everyone's job (including his) is ending...

Your 10 year-old gets his foot stuck under a kid during a soccer game and your little athlete who loves to run, jump, and play ends up in a wheelchair for 2 ½ months...

Your landlord comes to tell you that he's raising the rent by 30% now that the construction is done on his place...

And the business launch you all were planning on, to replenish the bank account and carry you through for a while, ends up a bust and clearing out what's left of your resources?

You do what any other red-blooded, perimenopausal, on-the-verge-of-a-nervous-breakdown woman in her late 40's would do...

You go to Italy.

Okay, it wasn't quite that smooth a transition.

First, I was pissed. I mean really, really, uber-goober, dropped the f-bomb (like, a lot) while doing Italian Therapy (a.k.a "cleaning baseboards" like, a lot) to get my "Holy crap, what is going on with my life???" frustrations out,

Pissed.

Like, a lot.

(I know. I already said that.)

It was intense and I was having a middle-age meltdown when, honestly...I just got tired of it. I don't do anger well -- I'm just not super comfortable with that emotion. And so, because it takes a lot of energy to be that mad at this thing called "Life", I decided to take a different tack...

I laid in my bed, stared at the ceiling (where I'm pretty sure God lives) and I asked one question, in three parts:

What would I do if time, money, and opportunity were no object?

I'd close my eyes, take a deep breath, and then, I'd just start to dream. In the space of "Nothing is wrong and anything is possible" -- this is what I came up with...

I want to get rid of a lot of stuff -- sell it, give it away, throw it out -- and then, I want to pack up what's left, put it in storage and put my kids in the car for an epic road trip.

I want to do a book tour, connecting with my readers, who have become friends on social media, from all around the country. I just want to spend time with them -- doing workshops and coaching sessions and have a real "together" time.

Then, I want to buy one-way tickets to Europe and take off -- just go and explore -- especially Italy -- and console myself with gelato, music, and art and some more gelato.

I want us all to heal from the pain we've gone through and I want us to feel connected to our souls, our purpose, and each other again. We will do all this and more -- and we'll call it our "Magical, Healing Adventure."

That was my dream.

———————————

I guess that's what I've done a lot in life: Taken a super weird, mundane, painful, or unexpected circumstance and either dug out the treasure or turned it into magic, and healing, and an adventure.

Whether it was turning off almost all of the breakers in our house.

Taking the TV out of our home 20 years ago.

Or

Traveling across the country or across "The Pond."

We have lived a very Unconventional Life.

Taking chances that the average bear wouldn't take for some very good, sound, and sane reasons.

But we did it anyway.

I remember the wonderful Jewish philosopher, Edwin Friedman, who said that our brain can only imagine so far -- at some point we need to get up and risk adventure.

To hop on the plane -- or jump out of it --
To skinny dip in the pond,
To put all your money on "21 black"
To love again after we have been hurt.

"Risking adventure" has taken on various forms in our lives.

You should know right now: it never goes as planned.

Like Italy: no one told me that gelato and wine would become the drugs of choice when I was going through our family identity crisis. And that, no matter how lost I felt on the streets in Florence, it would be nothing compared to my deep wish for a roadmap to help my youngest son find his way back to his soul.

But like no one could ever prepare you for the challenges, no one could ever prepare you for the unexpected gifts that come from getting lost and ending up where you never really knew you needed to be, in order to find yourself again.

These pages are filled with 21 chapters (because it's my favorite number), filled with vignettes of where messes and magic collide. Where the divine spark happens in the middle of the madness and instead of jumping off the ledge you're standing on, you find yourself awake to your inspiration and intuition again --

And able to fly.

There are some things you should know before you read on:

These are in no particular time or location sequence (except for a couple where it made the most sense) so, if in one chapter my children are teenagers in California and the next chapter they are toddlers in New York, just reset yourself into the new time and locale. I purposely left their ages in the text so that you could understand why I was exhausted, hiding under the covers, or drinking copious amounts of Sauvignon Blanc.

Most of these adventures were done with no savings in the bank, no promise of a certain income, and both of us driving cars that averaged 18 years-old. There is no silver spoon or massive amount of money required to dream. My method was: Dream first and dream strong, commit yourself to your vision and (eventually) everything you need will appear. Usually in some mind-boggling, miraculous way that becomes your oxygen. Breathing in miracles with a mindset that says "anything is possible" will become your new atmosphere.

There are several spiritual and religious beliefs and vernacular in some of the chapters. Personally, my spiritual journey has been some of the biggest grist for my mill and trust me, I have wanted to hide the off-putting, pain-in-the-ass, judgmental parts that I have gone through so that I could just seem as enlightened and awake as I am now (cough, cough).

But instead of hiding it or shading it in a way that makes it all sound the same, I've decided to let the colors be as bold or dark, or neutral as they were for that time because the process matters. I've gone from Catholicism to Born-Again-Christianity, down the roads of Buddhism, Taoism, Sufism, Gnosticism, Humanism, and Veganism (made you look) to where I landed today at my current beliefs:

God is Love and so are we, and I eat bacon.

I call God many names: Love, Spirit, The Divine, and "Words with No Voice" (because I mostly hear words with no voice as a part of my spiritual communication). I also call God "He" for the sake of ease and flow in the sentences -- if I start writing He/She/It every time I want to mention the Divine, at some point you will grow weary and it will run together and sound like "He Shit" in your head and that's not really the vibe I was going for.

And, by the way: I swear. Not a lot, but enough to either make you feel a little more understood or a little uncomfortable. Either way, don't miss the stories. They're worth their weight in gold.

I love the people in these vignettes. They are all real but, in some cases, their names aren't. That was to protect the innocent: namely, me.

The ones whose names and lives matter the most are my husband, Rock, and our two sons, Caleb and Seth - whom I affectionately refer to as "Thing 1" and "Thing 2" (we didn't call them that until after they saw Dr. Seuss and loved it.) They are my biggest teachers and the reason for me writing these stories out in full: because I wanted them to have records of the life that they've lived, the lessons we've learned, and the lineage of the miracles they are part of -- and I wanted you to meet these two hilarious sages who have taught me so much more than I could have imagined when I was walking into Costco and buying diapers...*again.*

Enjoy the journey and the imperfections -- my hope is that the heart and spirit will grab you in a way that reminds you of the greatness that is alive in you and in life -- that you can find treasures in unexpected places, and that your power is alive and well to be the Alchemist: to take whatever isn't as you wish it were, and turn it into gold.

I'm so glad we get to share these pages together.

Welcome to my Unconventional Life.

It wouldn't be the same without you.

- Stacey Robbins

Seal Beach, CA June 2017

1

Tales from an MRI Tube

Dizzy, when you're 40, isn't as much fun as it sounds.

No one really knew why I was getting this stumbling, drunk-feeling brain that wasn't really spinning but mostly just lost in space. My face would turn the color of school glue and my eyes would shimmy back and forth. The doctors told me the official word for the eye-thing was "nystagmus."

The kids were young and I was scared.

After trips to the ER, the doctors, and a scrillion different expensive tests to rule out the easier things, my doctor looked at me and said, "It's time for an MRI. We need to rule out some other possibilities..."

I knew the "possibilities" she was talking about and it made me lose my breath.

Rock's job was new and he felt he couldn't leave for a few hours to take me to the test. Part of me understood and part of me hated him. I kissed my boys good-bye that morning, feeling alone inside myself and wondering which version of mommy they were going to see when I came home: The relieved mommy, the waiting-for-news mommy, or the mommy who just had a faithquake -- whose life would never be the same.

I don't know how I drove myself, between what was going on in my brain and the turmoil in my head, but I did.

Halfway there, I pulled over on the side of the 73 Toll Road to take a pause. I got out of the car and leaned my hands onto my knees -- closed my eyes and breathed in. When I opened them, I was struck by the rolling green hills in a new way. January was always full of vibrant color in Southern California after our winter rains had started. I sent up a prayer for some strength and it was at that moment that my friend, Brad, called. He was one of the publishers I was working with on a possible new venture and he just happened to reach out at the perfect moment to talk me through the rest of my drive. I was so grateful for the timing.

Brad and I hung up just as I was about to walk in the door to my appointment. I smiled weakly as I handed my paperwork to the woman at the front desk who smiled warmly at me.

I'm sure it wasn't the first time that someone had looked to her seeking comfort in exchange for paperwork.

A girl who was at least a decade younger than me, with a natural, blonde ponytail came out in scrubs and holding a chart, "Mrs. Robbins?" I nodded, "My name is Sarah and I'll be doing your MRI today."

At the risk of being the oddest duck she'd ever met, I followed her to the changing area and started in with my questions: "Hi, Sarah. Can you do me a big favor when I go into the room with the MRI?"

She turned and smiled and nodded in a "Go ahead and tell me, but I can't promise you anything" kind of way.

"Well, could you walk me in backwards with my eyes closed?"

I know it sounds crazy but I had read that it's best to not see how big the machine is and how small the tube is, when you're dealing with claustrophobia -- which I was -- on top of the dizziness.

She thought for a second and said, "I'm not sure I can do that, Mrs. Robbins. I think you have to walk in with your eyes open for liability purposes." I sighed, trying to think of something...

"Well, what would you do if I were blind?" (My husband would be giving himself brain damage from rolling his eyes if he were here, listening to me ask these questions.)

Sarah paused again, "Well, we'd have to roll you in a wheelchair."

I considered that for a second, "Okay then, Can you roll me into the room backwards."

She stared at me to see if I was joking.

I wasn't.

"Ummm... well, no, Mrs. Robbins. But I can roll you in forward -- and you can close your eyes."

Rocky would have had to turn away and bite his tongue at this point of my ridiculousness.

I didn't even get to ask her my other questions like, "What happens if there's an earthquake while I'm in the middle of the test?" and "Have you ever had a power outage while someone's in the tube?" and my favorite one that I don't dare to ask but really, really want to, "Has the machine ever collapsed on someone while they're inside?"

It's probably better he didn't come...

I didn't need someone else witnessing my default behavior in life, "If it's scary, close your eyes and pretend it's not there."

And all my scrillions of examples:

I'm sure if you don't open that piece of scary IRS tax mail on the counter, it will just go away.
I'm sure if you avoid your blood test, your health will improve.
I'm sure if you don't look at the scale after the three-week cheese and chocolate-palooza, you won't have gained weight.

Yeah, only one problem: Life doesn't actually work that way. Even when you want to convince yourself it could.

Sarah got the wheelchair and rolled me in (with my eyes closed, thank you very much) and helped me get situated on the table. She asked me all the identifying questions to make sure I was who I said I was, which kind of makes me laugh. Is there really someone who would actually WANT to pretend to be me right now? Is there really someone out there who gets such a thrill from removing all of their metal items so that they could spend what feels like a lifetime, in a small, hollow, metal tube that I didn't even want to see -- let alone be in?

Movies have stunt doubles. I'd actually welcome an MRI double -- but I'm pretty sure there's not a category for that in the yellow pages.

Sarah laid me down on the metal conveyor belt that would eventually slide me inside the chamber -- but first, had to put my head into a device that's sort of an umpire's mask meets Hannibal Lecter meets batting cage -- kind of apparatus.

My claustrophobia was escalating and I wasn't even in the tube yet.

"I don't think I can do this, Sarah." I said feeling short of breath.

She patted my arm, "You can do this Mrs. Robbins."

I had a feeling this wasn't going to be the last time we had that little exchange.

But she didn't understand:

I was dizzy.
And scared.
I had kids and I wanted to dance with them at their weddings.
I had a husband I wanted to bitch at for not coming with me today, and then, make up and share a bottle of red wine together, tonight... and then, hopefully, at some point, in Italy.

It all felt so strange and impersonal...

"Please, Sarah, call me, 'Stacey.'"

She smiled, "Okay, Stacey."

I took a deep breath and started meditating:

I breathe in holy peace, I breathe out fear.

I closed my eyes as Sarah gave me the instructions:

"Now, Mrs. Robbins, I mean, *Stacey*... we're doing two MRI's today -- one of your brain and one of your neck."

I breathe in holy peace, I breathe out fear.

"So, it's kind of an extra long test today. The first portion will take about an hour and then, we'll roll you out, inject you with the contrast dye and the last part will be 45 minutes."

I breathe in, Holy shit - I breathe out there is no freakin' way...

I felt myself starting to hyperventilate.

My meditation practice definitely needed some more work.

"Get me out of here, Sarah!" I desperately called out toward the speaker above my face, after the first test started. Yeah. My relatively new meditation practice wasn't cutting it.

I swear to Hermes: The MRI machine was filled with jackhammers instead of magnets because that's what it sounded like. A ton of jackhammers, banging straight into my head.

My head stuck in a cage
The cage and I stuck inside the MRI tube
With a million freaking jackhammers.

Sarah rolled me out, not fast enough, and opened the cage so that I could sit up.

I bent forward and buried my swimming head into my hands -- trying to comfort myself between the trifecta of dizzy, scared, and alone.

God, please help. Please, please, help me.

Help.

God.
Please...

When I lifted my head out of my hands, I glanced up and what I saw took my breath away:

There was a massive window in front of me, the size of the entire wall, and all you could see were the deepest-colored, green-covered trees all around the woods.

I sighed the deepest sigh, and smiled. It was such an unexpected comfort to see so much nature and life all around me. I breathed in the trees, reminded that they have a gift of taking our carbon dioxide that we breathe out and turning it into the oxygen that we breathe in. I closed my eyes again and this time could see the trees in my mind's eye.

I can do this, I told myself.

The voice inside me said:
I need to do this. I need to know what's going on. The boys need to have their mommy back. And I need to have my peace.

But then, I heard words come to me from some Divine place:

Peace isn't going to come when you have an answer. Peace is what you need to have while you're on the way to the answer.

I knew it was true. I could feel it in my soul.

God, please help me. Please...I can't do this without help right now. I heard my heart plead.

Three prayerful thoughts came to me while I was sitting in front of the Counsel of the Sacred Forest.

Can you please make the jackhammers sound like music?
Can you please give me others to pray for, who are in greater need than I am?
Can you please tell me something in that tube that I wouldn't hear anywhere else --

That this would be like a sanctuary for me.

That's what I sent out to the Universe. The prayer of the trees felt spacious and alive in me.

I lifted my head toward the technologist, "I can do this, Sarah. Let's do this."

She nodded, reassuringly, while I scooched my body onto my back. Sarah locked my head in place, and the machine slid me in.

The jackhammers started, but they didn't sound like that after about a minute. They twisted and turned and transformed into some kind of Middle Eastern, angelic, transcendent song. It had the trip-out effect of being on a drug, only it was some weird mystical melody that soothed me
instead.

After a time of settling into the sounds around me, I moved my hands up the line of my body toward my solar plexus and took a centering breath in. It was time to pray. People starting coming to my heart and mind. My long-time friend Peter, diagnosed with ALS -- and dear, sweet Sandra -- Chuck's wife, pregnant with their third child, had ALS, too. My heart ached for those friends and my soul called out on their behalf. Other names like Jean and Stephen, Mary and Al and others came to me as I prayed prayer after prayer for my friends in need. Sarah's voice was somewhere in the far-off distance, telling me that she was going to bring me out and the nurse was going to inject the dye.

In the haze of the music and prayers, the conveyor belt brought me back in as I now placed my hand over my abdomen -- the place of my womb, where life comes from -- and I asked God to show me something here that I wouldn't know if I were anywhere else.

I heard Words with No Voice (the name that I call "God") say to me:

"If you knew your true identity, you would walk in the power that I have already given you."

With those words there came a picture: Of me, walking through town and everywhere I walked and everywhere I looked, my name was appearing. Every sign that I saw and every store had my name on it - *every place was my own.* I owned it. I owned everything. If I needed something, I didn't walk in some place, hoping or begging or wishing that someone would source me with it -- no, I was the resource and I walked with confidence, because I knew that what I needed would be within my reach.

I wasn't beholden to anyone. I was beholding everything.

The posture was completely different. To know who I was allowed me to live differently in my vision. Humble, Grateful, Confident, Assured...

Me.
I felt myself smile while the twisting music wrapped around me.

"Mrs. Robbins -- shoot. I mean, Stacey? The test is over. You did it -- you're done!" Sarah's voice came through the speaker and I swear that I heard her voice swell with pride. The churning sound of the conveyor brought me out into the light.

After the clicking and unlatching of the head cage, I sat up and looked out at the trees. They had been so good to me and helped me to be brave.

"Thank you," I whispered to them.

"You're welcome," Sarah answered as she turned in her swivel chair. I smiled and my eyes met hers for the first time since we were introduced almost three hours ago. Really looked at her. Not with a need for her to comfort me or assure me -- but with a gratitude.

I could give her my gratitude.

Not because the MRI was over,
But because I had an encounter where jackhammers turned to music, and anxiety turned to prayers, and neediness turned to confidence -- Not in a church full of steeples and ceremonies --
But in a small magnetic tube that became my sanctuary.

The place where I met God and God met me -- not just with the getting through the test so that I could be done,

But getting through to me
In that tight, little space
So that I could know who I was
So that I could have peace

So that I could be free.

2
It's a "Beautiful" Thing

"You're so beautiful, funny, smart, strong, generous, loving, and gifted..."

It sounds like the affirmations of Saturday Night Live character, Stuart Smalley. His needy, lispy voice encouraging his reflection in the mirror to get laughs from the live audience, and to convince himself out of his neurosis -- always ending with the infamous phrase, "And doggone it, people like me."

But before he ever came on the scene, these were the words my parents spoke to me.

About *me*.

It was the list I could practically recite myself with a "blah, blah, blah" on the end when I was a teenager and I wasn't buying it -- because you know, parents are "weird."

But the truth is: I was all of those things.

I ended up starting my own business -- a professional music career -- at age 15. I was well-read, could do great impressions of comedians that would leave my family peeing in their pants -- and we turned heads, all five of us, when we'd walk into a restaurant.

My whole Italian family was beautiful. Crazy? Yes. A little extra in the fanny? Yes. A little signature Sicilian bump on the nose? Yes. And could go from zero to bitchy in about a second?

Hell, yes.

But always beautiful.

And I didn't realize how important beauty was to me, until it went away.

I think it was likely the perfect storm of circumstances in my life that landed me with Hashimoto's Thyroiditis -- the autoimmune dis-ease that attacks your thyroid and messes with every cell in your body. The stress of my household growing up (my parents weren't always spouting my positive attributes, trust me), the gobs of secret trauma I had gone through as a child outside of the home, and the very fundamentalist religious belief I chose to "save" me from all of that trauma (with a punishing God included, no extra charge).

All of those set me up perfectly to become a perfectionist, workaholic, who was uber-hard on herself, felt guilty all the time, and rarely gave herself any slack.

I didn't really have any sense of rest and peace.

"Peace" for me, was having my house look good, my reputation look good, and my body look good.

"Peace" wasn't an inside state of being, coming from an inner state of acceptance and contentment.

No way.

My thoughts were going about a scrillion miles an hour about "what a failure I was" and if I could just figure out that one thing to do better -- *then*, I could finally be "good enough" and relax.

I was like that duck in the water that looks like it's gliding but is paddling like crazy underneath the water's surface.

That was me.

Eventually, at around 27 years-old, it all caught up with me: The stress from the past, the current stressful marriage, the ridiculous work schedule I had with a demanding music career, two car accidents, and losing my dad to diabetes when he was 49.

I found myself changing. Not just moody or bitchy or tired. I mean, yes, all those things, but my body changed too.

I had gained a little weight in the past, but had always been able to do some ridiculous fad or crash diet, with a little extra exercise to get it off in a blink.

Not this time.

This time, I was gaining 10-15 lbs. in a month and no amount of dieting or working with my personal trainer was getting it off.

The scale was creeping up. And sometimes leaping up.

I felt so out of control.

I went to my doctor.

He put me on three times the dose of Fen-Phen to lose weight.

(Remember Fen-Phen? Remember when it was going through all the scrutiny from giving people mitral-valve prolapse? Yeah. I was on three times the regular dose. Insert eye-rolling here).

Still gaining weight. Only this time with anxiety attacks from the medication and the still undiagnosed thyroid disease.

My scale kept climbing:

175.
180.
185.

My legs got so dry, they looked like the Sahara.

195.

I lost 1/3 of my eyebrows. I looked like an inflated Mr. Spock on Star Trek.

Not my best look.

The scale reached that unbelievable number 200 and I was pretty sure that the ground trembled at the thought of me getting out of bed each day.

I worked out even harder with my personal trainer and wrote down every bite of food.

205.
210.
215.

My hair stopped growing on my legs. I said to my husband, "I think I'm getting fatter, faster than my hair can grow."

We laughed for a second. But only a second 'cause I was kind of serious.

I went to doctor after doctor. Specialist after specialist.
At least 10 in that year.

Everyone scratched their heads.

I felt like Larry, Moe, and Curly were my medical team that year.

Some of them told me I was dying.
Several told me that if I lived, I'd never have children.

I was depressed.
I was getting fatter.

But not just that, I was getting uglier, too.

My hair turned Bozo-The-Clown orange (not kidding) and became as rough as a Brillo pad.

My face got welts and scabs all over it.

My arms looked like someone had pricked me with a pin. If you touched my skin, it would literally bleed.

I tipped the scales (or so I thought) at 240 by the time I collapsed in pain, while working in the school where I was teaching music. A colleague took me to a local urgent care. The doctor took blood work that the other doctors had failed to take or to see clearly.

She called me a few days later, "Mrs. Robbins: The bad news is you have hypothyroidism. Your TSH is 19.0. The good news is, we'll put you on medication and you'll be back to your normal weight in three months."

I swear, I heard the angels sing.

I was so relieved. I was going to get to not only *be* me again but *look* like me again.

I took the meds faithfully, exercised regularly and gained 30 more pounds in three months.

I'm not kidding.

I was 270 lbs.

I looked like I ate myself.

I'd walk past the windows of the businesses and see the reflection of my huge self and I'd stop.

That couldn't be me.

Where did I go?

Shit.

The sales people who used to walk right up to me when I was skinny, now ignored me in the store.

The days of people asking my husband and me if we were models, were traded for people rudely telling him, "You can do better."

Right in front of me.

I'm not sure I can completely express how completely this completely sucked. And how horribly fat people are sometimes treated when they're not being ignored.

Here I went from "beautiful" being at the top of my list, to not anywhere on it. But not only that, I had to confront one of the biggest things I didn't even know I needed to address:

I had to look at how I had made being beautiful so important to my identity.

That it wasn't just an adjustment in my looks that I was dealing with. At some point, I had to have the honest conversation, about how I had allowed myself to believe the press I had received my whole life:

That being beautiful meant you were worth more.

More worthy of love
And respect
And kind treatment
And attention
And good service
And a good life.

I was getting the opportunity (which didn't feel like an opportunity at the time, trust me) to examine my crappy thinking

And to love me.
Unconditionally.

I didn't do that.
I didn't love me unconditionally.

I thought that because I had a successful business, and a great reputation, and an attractive appearance, that I was credible.

That whole list I had grown up with had turned from a list of affirmations, to a standard of acceptability.

If I was funny
If I was smart
If I was gifted
If I was beautiful...

then,

I could be loved.

They had become terms of agreement in my heart instead of qualities I possessed.

So, when I had lost my sense of humor and started to stutter (because it can actually affect your speech when your brain is so toxic from an underactive thyroid)

and when I couldn't provide financially and I couldn't perform

and I definitely
wasn't
beautiful,

I didn't believe that I was worth loving.

When all those qualities went away, I didn't know who I was.

It became my journey to examine those beliefs of what made me valuable: Where they came from and how to shift to a more internal, and eternal perspective on my worth.

———————

While all of this was going on, a strange, other, side story was in the works (that I have been given complete permission to share): My husband had issues with pornography since he was a teen and his mom had died. He used it to cope with the pain. I didn't know about this until after we got married when I was 20. It felt so rejecting. There I was, 135 pounds and sexy and his eyes were everywhere but on me.

We went through seven years like that. For anyone who's had a partner with an addiction (or what we call a "compulsion" in our house) you know that the days are very, very long.

And seven years feels like a lifetime.

In the middle of me being really sick and really fat, the weirdest thing happened:

My husband got over the issues with pornography.

When I was at my heaviest.
My bitchiest.
My lowest libido-est.
There *he* was, loving *me*.
Adoring *me*.

He was doing a whole lot of inner work and I was 270 lbs. -- looking and feeling like a beached whale -- and his heart started turning toward me. He would look at me like I was the only woman on the planet.

I'd lie on the bed on my side, he'd stroke my big hips and say, "You are so so beautiful."

And I would look behind me to see who he was talking to.

It was *me*.

He was seeing and loving

me!

Do you know what a great story that is?

(Even though it sounds like an awful lot of information for not really knowing me.)

It's a great story because it showed me that love is about a *heart* that see things differently and not about a woman who has herself put together perfectly.

How many nights before I had gotten sick had I asked myself,

"What do *I* need? Smaller hips? Bigger boobs? A kinder disposition? Should I cook more, act more docile, be more social?"

"What did *he* need? More sex, less conflict? More money, more time, more toys?"

I was looking for the magic formula that was going to make him love me.

Me + skinny + pretty + unbitchy = love

But what if I did all that and *then* he left pornography?

I would never have been able to trust his love.

And I would always be the manager of his fidelity: because if I could change and make him faithful, then I could change and make him unfaithful. I didn't want that job and couldn't afford that kind of devotion.

His love would be based on my performance instead of his commitment to love me.

When he left pornography in the middle of me being at my *worst*, When I was literally too sick to change my circumstances... I knew that I could trust him to love me at my *best*.

I needed that message sent to me.
I needed to *live* that message inside of *me*.

My husband's heart changed for me when he faced and healed his issues.

That was the wake up call that my heart needed, too.

Because I needed to do that work in me, so that I could shift and love me...

For me

For who I was
And
For where I was.

I went on that journey for a few years and it was deep and confrontational -- but god, it was so freaking rewarding.

I learned to appreciate my internal qualities like my integrity, character, wisdom, and grace.

And yes, I took care of myself externally instead of doing that whole "waiting until I'm skinny to take care of myself" bullshit. I've done that before during my heavier times -- where I hid in dark clothing with ratty hair, and no makeup because I wasn't at my best weight.

In the space of that, I got connected to the practitioners who would guide me with those same qualities that I was appreciating in myself. I got the healing meds and foods going, which helped my metabolism work on my behalf instead of against me, all while learning more about the intricacies of Hashimoto's.

Maybe because I had started working FOR me, instead of AGAINST me.

I'm not doing that anymore.

Well, not as much, anyway.

It's a little bit of a process.

I attended a class years ago and someone asked me, "What would you do if you were your goal weight?"

I got that weird faraway look in my eyes like I was talking about a unicorn or something:

"I'd wear cute clothes. Laugh, without worrying about a double, or triple chin appearing. And I'd dance with my kids without worrying about the size of my butt."

The teacher said to me, "The secret to getting there, is doing that stuff *now*. Live your life *now*. Don't wait for your idea of "perfect" in order to live a self-expressed life."

So, I laugh

Now.

And I dance

Now.

And I put on cute clothes instead of my family threatening to nominate me for the show "What Not to Wear."

Now.

I'm not done but I am different.

My thighs aren't as big as they were, but they're not as small as they once were either.

I love my thighs. Even though they remind me of a Shar Pei puppy sometimes, these legs have faithfully carried me through life.

My arms might be flappy underneath, but they are the arms my children run to because they know that love is there and that I will not hesitate to wrap them up in that embrace.

And I let my husband ravish me with his love, as we celebrate our 28th anniversary this year, even though old mental tapes sometimes tell me I don't deserve it. Because the truth is this: I *am* smart and funny. I *am* gifted and generous. I *am* loving and strong.

And doggone it,

I like me.

And *that* is what makes me
Beautiful.

3
The Cellulite is Right Where I Left It

I had been on the diet for four weeks. It was one of those gut-busting, eat-no-fat, have-no-fun kind of diets. One of the hundreds I had tried since I was 10 and thought I was fat, when I really wasn't.

Now I was in my 30's and really was "fat." A thyroid problem, plus having two children less than 2 years apart, had made my metabolism crawl like a slug on a cold winter's day. I'm sure there were other reasons that contributed to it, but ultimately it felt like I'd sent out invitations for every bit of cellulite to come to a neighborhood party on my thighs

And everyone RSVP'd an enthusiastic, "Yes!"

And then, brought their friends.

Oh.
Joy.

While standing by my closet, I dropped my sweat pants to my ankles. With only my granny panties showing, I asked my husband, "Can you look at this?"

I could feel his eyes widening in that, "Uh oh, what game am I going to play and lose today?" kind of way.

He made his way slowly across the room and, with a bit of hesitation asked, "What's up?"

I pointed to the back of my thighs and my butt in a pleading way:

"Is there less cellulite than before?"

He looked at me, took a deep breath, and then, knelt down behind me. I twisted my upper body around and peeked, as he squinched his eyes and poured over every inch of my legs. I was losing oxygen to contort my body for so long, so I turned around to face my clothes hanging in front of me. I closed my eyes and exhaled the breath I didn't realize I was holding.

You can't suck in cellulite, Stacey, I reminded myself in my head.

My husband was quiet, except for the occasional, "Hmmm…" After about 60 seconds (which is a long time to have someone examining your nether regions in broad daylight) I started wiggling like a three-year-old doing the "Pee-Pee" dance.

"Please, Rock, please, tell me: Is there less cellulite than there used to be?"

He stood up, sighed, and put one hand on his hip while the other pointed toward my legs like Vanna White pointing to the letter "A" on the board,

"Babe, I didn't even know you *had* cellulite. I honestly have no clue what you're talking about."

I scanned his face, searching for a drop of, "There's really a Titanic amount of adipose tissue down there, but I don't dare say a word" in his eyes. None. Not even a speck.

I shimmied my sweats back up, never taking my eyes off of his. "Really?" I looked in his eyes with a different vulnerability than it took to have him stare at my rear-end. This was me letting him see my insecurity that'd been swirling around in my soul.

He nodded and smiled. Rock rested his hands on my hips and pulled me close, "Really. I mean it. I'm not just saying that, hon." He tugged on my hips to make sure I was paying attention. "And no, I know what you're thinking: I don't need glasses or better lighting. I just don't see what you're talking about."

He wrapped his arms around me and swayed back and forth a bit, maybe to lull my fears out of me.

I let him hug me and I settled in -- in a different, less self-protective way -- as this flash of revelation came over me ...

All those times I had asked him to find the ketchup in the fridge, he'd open the door, bend over, look *allllll* around -- and not see it. I'd sigh in complete exasperation as I walked right to the spot where I said it was, pull it from the obvious place that God and everyone could see -- including blind people -- and he'd close the door.

He'd shake his head, not understanding how he had missed it. And I'd nearly have brain damage from rolling my eyes in frustration.

It happened so often that on one of our anniversaries he gave me a card. On the front, it was a husband sticking his head into a refrigerator that only had butter -- rows and rows of it -- on the door and every shelf...just completely lined with sticks and sticks of bright, yellow butter. In the next frame he is calling out to his wife in desperation, "Honey! Where's the butter?"

I giggled at the card 'cause it's funny, but rolled my eyes because, seriously -- it's my life.

And it didn't just stop at ketchup or the butter -- Rock also couldn't see the person who was driving like an ass and nearly hit my side of the car, or the sagging, stinky diaper that needed to be changed, or the bank account that needed to be balanced.

It took me a while, but today I finally understood for the first time -- that even though it was right in front of him, it just wasn't on his radar.

He misses things that I think range from "kinda important" to "really, really freaking important." But he also sees things that I don't. Like my beauty, despite my weight. And my charm, despite my crankiness. And my wisdom, despite my pride.

We're not the same. We're two different people. And when I stop expecting him to be like me and start celebrating him being like him, I stop being such a self-righteous pain in the ass who can actually enjoy the unique person that he is.

So, do I really think that I have no cellulite on my thighs? Hell, no. I took pictures of myself after he left the room and it's like ten Shar Pei puppies down there.

What I do know -- and now love -- is this: because it's not what matters to him, it's not what he sees.

And that because I really matter to him,
he sees *me*.

4
The Power of Choice

I met a man named Owen. He was all *guy,* red hair, and a face that you knew turned nearly purple when he was pissed. I was sitting next to him and he had a story that I needed to hear.

You see, Owen was a racecar driver. He had been driving in a particular race for 9 years. This was going to be his 10th – and his last – because after that, Owen was going to retire.

He had gone through some personal growth courses that year and hired a coach to walk him through the mind game portion as he approached his 10th race. You could tell, just by listening to Owen, that compliance wasn't his favorite sport. But he was embracing a new kind of willingness. Willing to try thinking another way than he had for the 9 years prior.

One of the things that really mattered was removing the self-sabotaging excuses that might affect him for the race. So, to make sure he had the right gear ready for the day, he called way ahead to the tire guy, Tom, to make sure that he had what Owen needed.

"Tom, man, I NEED to make sure you've got my tires on race day. Here's the thing, Tom: I need the roundest tires you got. I don't want nothing else but the roundest tires, man, you hear me?"

I'm listening to Owen and thinking: *Aren't **all** the racecar tires round?* I mean, I can't picture square Fred Flintstone tires being an option on the track.

Anyway, Tom tells Owen, "No problem, man. I got your back, O. It's all good. You just show up and I'll have the best tires waiting for you."

Great.

Owen's going through his checklist and a couple weeks before the race, calls Tom again. "Told you, O: I got your back. Your tires are set, man. Everything's good. See you at the track."

The big day comes. Owen gets to Tom who's standing there with a cigarette hanging out of his mouth, nods to Owen and starts rolling his tires off the truck. Owen's looking around to see if these are for someone else, but they're not. They're his. "WHAT THE F*#K IS THIS, TOM? WHAT THE F*#K ARE THESE F*#KING TIRES, TOM?"

Owen's not happy.

Owen's turning purple.

Tom shoves the tire down and grabs the cigarette from between his lips, and stabbing in the direction of his angry customer, "Owen, don't start with me, man. These are the tires you asked for, these are the tires you got. And these are the only ones I got for you. I don't got anything else, man."

Tom walks back into the cavern of the truck to get the rest of the tires.

Owen's pissed.

Swearing under his breath, kicking the air, pacing, and pissed. He grabs his phone out of his pocket and calls his mind-game coach. After explaining what's happening, the coach tells him:

"Choose the tires, Owen. You gotta *choose* the tires. You can't change 'em, so you gotta choose 'em."

He and the coach had been having a lot of those conversations in the last year so the concept was familiar to Owen but the practice of it, was not.

Owen stormed up to Tom who was standing inside the edge of the truck. Owen shut his eyes, took a deep inhale and said to Tom, "I choose those damn tires."

Owen shifted his eyes up to Tom who looked perplexed, "You *what*?"

Owen gritted his teeth and said it again, but louder, the dark red creeping up the sides of his cheeks, "I said, 'I CHOOSE those tires.'"

Tom, still not understanding, pulled out his box of cigarettes from his t-shirt pocket and started tapping them, "Well, yeah, Owen. 'Cause them the only damn tires I got for you."

Owen glared at Tom, "No! That's not why…" He gritted his teeth and said it one last time to him, "I choose them, because *they're mine!*"

The pit crew got the tires on. Owen got behind the wheel. Eventually, the race started and Owen took off.

His wheel was shimmying like it had never shimmied before. Owen had to hold on tight. He wanted to blame it all on Tom but he kept hearing his coach's voice in his head telling him, "Choose the tires, Tom. Choose the tires."

With the roar of the engines and in the heat of the race, Owen yelled over all of the noise outside and the noise in his head, over and over again, "I CHOOSE THESE TIRES! I CHOOSE THESE TIRES! I CHOOSE THESE G*DDAMN TIRES!!"

And Owen crossed the finish line,

retiring from racing

And winning the race.

It was a beautiful couch. One of my favorite colors: This buttery, creamy, melt-in-your mouth and *sigh* kind of colors. It was sitting there in the showroom, full of designer this-and-that, making all the little-girl, dollhouse-loving parts of me go ooh-and-ahh.

It was one of the bigger purchases I had made since paying off the birth of both of my children, followed by years of what seemed like an endless supply of diapers. I was beside myself: to be able to splurge on something that didn't include the words "Super-absorbent" and "leak-proof" in the description,

I was absolutely giddy.

After running a swatch over to our new home to make sure it matched the new paint on the new walls, I was ready. It was perfect and I couldn't have been more proud of myself at a job well done. Our new little space was going to be a great place for the boys to run outside and play while I enjoyed being inside and doing my writing in my sweet, sweet sanctuary.

I put the money down, tucked my swatch into my purse and headed home to wait for six weeks until it was delivered.

Christmas came in July that year when the delivery men carried it in. It filled the room to perfection and the moment they left, I sat down and leaned back with a deeply satisfied feeling that all was well with the world.

Who knew the power of a couch? Holy crow.

Not me.

Until now.

I was just settling in when two, little, excited boys came running from outside, "YAY!!! The new couch is here!" And they ran, jumped and catapulted themselves onto the new couch with their dirty, little feet and I heard myself say, in a voice that sounded distinctly like my mother's:

"GETYOURFEETOFFTHECOUCH!"

And that was the moment I realized:

Holy shit. I bought the wrong couch.

I closed my eyes, took a deep breath and sat back on the couch in a totally different way.

What was I thinking?
Did I forget that I had a 3 and a 5 year old?
Did I forget that we live in Southern California
and that we never wear shoes?

Did I forget I was a freakin' mom and that these are the years when you buy dark, washable pieces of everything instead of light, stainable ones?

Oh my god.

Where was my head?

Where is my heart??

I'm Italian, raised Catholic so, guilt is sort of a default setting in my system, but the self-condemnation I felt was over the top.

I felt like a complete failure
Over a couch.

To make matters worse, one of our family members stopped by. She has a million upsides but one of her downsides is that she can make you feel like an idiot, even on a good day.

This was not a good day.

In the space of my not-shining moment, she didn't miss a beat, "You bought *this* couch? With *these* boys?" Then, she made a face at me and rolled her eyes.

Oh my god. Somebody shoot me.

Just take me out back and put me out of my misery.

It was that pain of feeling so much guilt. That punch in the gut, like you're a really bad mom for spending a healthy portion of the tax refund on something that doesn't work for two of the most important people in your world.

Even though you feed your kids organic food, always double check their seatbelts, and kiss them at least ten times before bed even though you're ready to fall on the floor with exhaustion,

Not to mention the other scrillion consciously *good* things you've done since they were in utero until this moment,

None of that good stuff mattered right now.

The evidence was in: You're just selfish. And wrong. Just very selfish and wrong.

I sat deeply in that thought for days while I sat stiffly on the edge of the couch, tormenting myself.

Until I remembered Owen and those damn tires.

"I choose this couch." I heard myself saying.

"I choose this couch." I said it again.

I repeated those words over and over again with a different emphasis on each word,

"*I* choose this couch."

"I *choose* this couch."

"I choose *this* couch."

"I choose this *couch*."

Until those words settled inside of me and I settled down.

The minute I did, two things happened:

A scrillion options popped in my head on what we could do with the couch:

We could slipcover it.
We could throw sheets on during the day when the boys are awake and take them off at night for my husband and me.
We could move it to the garage and build a man-cave for my husband (you know, as you normally would with a buttercream couch.)
We could donate it for a tax deduction.
We could sell it on Craigslist.

Suddenly, I had options.

And a dream.

Because the second thing that happened was a new vision for a new piece of furniture: an oversized, brown, leather couch from Pottery Barn.

I smiled.

The couch was still here but the problem of it -- and all the shame about it -- was gone.

———————

Resisting the situation I was in wasn't getting me out of it any faster.

How many times was it going to take me to learn that? Not just about the couch, but about my thighs, and my bank account, and the things I wanted my husband to do differently...

How many years had I lived that lesson already: how wishing something were different, and feeling awful about myself doesn't get me any closer to where I want to be?

Not with my weight
or my parenting
or my kitchen sink full of dishes.

If I could have made money by feeling badly about myself, I would have my own private island off the coast of Somewhere Fabulous.

I needed to retire from that unpaid, unrewarding career.

Choosing where I was at was the magic of the Chinese Finger Trick that used to make me crazy when I was a kid. We'd walk down to avenue and visit the "Five and Dime" store in New Jersey where I grew up. There were baskets filled with hundreds of toys and candies you could buy for a silver coin, and in one of them was this little woven, wicker cylinder. You put a finger in each end and give a slight tug and within about half a second, you were stuck.

The instinct when you're stuck is to pull harder because you just assume that getting your fingers out would mean just take them out. Duh.

Not with this.

After you're sweating and feeling that awful finger-claustrophobia that starts to spread into your chest and makes you want to cry and maybe even scream a little, someone has mercy on you and whispers, "You push your finger *in*" and then, you do and the space opens up and you're free.

This isn't about a couch or tires -- It's about every place in life that I beat myself up for not being good enough or better. It's about every mistake I make, every meltdown my kids have in a restaurant, every night I didn't sleep the amount of hours I thought I should, every wrinkle on my face that surprises me too soon, every political election that gets screwy, every meal that gets burnt, every person who acts like an ass when I think they should be kind, and pretty much just...

everything.

When I choose life, the way it is -- and the way that it is not -- instead of wishing it were different and wishing I were a better person about it all, something opens up from that tight space inside of me, and I find myself free.

Like with the couch.

Ah yes, the couch...

We listed the couch on Craigslist and sold it to a more-than-middle-aged couple who had just bought a cottage at the beach. They were thrilled to get our treasure for a song and we were thrilled to get our life with dirty feet back.

As for us, a couple of days after I chose the couch, we went for a walk down the street to my friend Amy's. My boys loved playing with her boys. We walked into her house and it was like a furniture factory exploded in there.

"Amy. What the heck is going on?"

She rolled her eyes, "Well, we bought a new couch for the house, a new couch for the studio and then, we sold our cabin in the mountains and we got the couch from up there and we already had two couches…"

She pointed to this big, comfy-looking, brown, leather couch that came from the mountain home. I said, "Ames, oh my gosh. I love that couch."

"Yeah. We got it from Pottery Barn – the outlet that sells it for a little less when it has a dent or something. This one has a small tear in the back but you can't even see it." She rolled her eyes again. "My friend promised to pick it up three times to take it off my hands, but she never shows up."

I was still staring at the couch, "Honey, I'll buy it from you, if she doesn't want it."

Amy shook her head, "Oh god, no. Please. If you'll just take it today, you can have it."

That night, my husband accompanied by Thing 1 and Thing 2 strolled down the street singing songs from Amy's house, like a scene out of The Monkees, with a big brown, Pottery Barn leather couch on rollers, coming straight to our door.

The power of choosing.

How did Owen win the race? He chose the tires.
How did I get the couch I really wanted? I chose the couch I had.

How do I get through this place, whatever place it is in my life where I feel stuck and like I'm never, ever, *ever* going to get free?

I take a deep breath, move myself a little closer rather than far away, stop beating myself up...

and choose it.

Afterthoughts on The Power of Choice

My husband has the concept of choosing me down to perfection.

But I didn't figure that out for a long time. I was too distracted by trying to change him, to really notice that he was just busy accepting me.

Me and my cellulite.
Me and my crankiness.
Me and my health condition.

I was busy criticizing my voice for being too smooth and simple when I sang and he was busy enjoying it.

I was busy criticizing my body for being too heavy and he was busy enjoying it.

Wishing something were different than it is, steals the joy right out of it.

Acceptance, it's such a beautiful thing.

Seth asked me when he was 11, "What advice would you give to yourself if you were my age?"

I love his questions, they're absolutely delicious. And the fact that he thinks Indiana is in India is kinda cute, too.

I said to him, "I would spend more time enjoying who I was instead of wishing I were different so that other people would like me. I would focus on liking me and being true to my heart and not worrying if anyone understood me or not."

He nodded. The sage in him gets it.

I remember writing a poem to my husband, that I read to him one night:

"Do you love me … even though …

Even though I used to be younger and skinny
But now I'm older and kinda zig-zaggy?

I used to zip around and get a lot of things done
But now, I get the laundry done …
Occasionally?

I used to not have so many cares in the world
But now, I get a little overwhelmed and cranky?

Do you love me, even though …?"

He looked in my eyes, "Honey, I didn't start loving you because you did those things so, I don't stop loving you when you don't."

He pulled me close and had those little crinkly, smile lines on the side of his eyes so, I knew something good was coming,

"I just love you because you're *mine*."

He doesn't spend his energy resisting who I am and where I'm at.

I've spent a lot of energy resisting me.

Rock and Byron Katie would get along swimmingly. Byron is an amazing thought leader and author, who tells her journey from being resistant to being free. She wrote in her book "Loving What Is", "I no longer have to work to let go of my negative thoughts, I greet them with understanding, and then they let go of me."

There is something about the whole idea of letting go of The Way We Thought Life Should Be and getting to embrace Life as It Is and It is Not.

My teenagers remind me of this all the time and honestly, they make me a little nervous. They ask questions about sex and "what does this slang word mean" -- and queries about life or death,

And holy shit ...

Every bit of button-pushing on the places that are unhealed, unknowing, or shameful for me -- that I resist inside of me -- I end up tempted to resist outside of me, too.

But if their curiosity is met with shame -- the way mine was when I was a curious child -- then, I'm just passing the shame on.

I'm not excited about leaving a legacy of shame.

I'm really excited about leaving a Legacy of Love.

So, if I do something different than my shameful instinct to resist, and I choose life for what it is, I can engage it from a brain and heart that are present and peaceful and full of love -- instead of hearing that screechy "DANGER WILL ROBINSON!!" kind of shit that makes my heart race and my feet want to run like I'm being chased by a bear.

Pressing in, instead of resisting.
Accepting, instead of blaming.
Choosing, instead of regretting.

If I want to live in "a world that works for everyone" as my spiritual center states in its mission, then, that means that I need to live in my inner world -- in a heart, body, and a mindset, that works for me.

That means that in order to choose you, in all of your mix of greatness and flaws and foibles,

I have to be willing ...
To choose *me*.

5
Do What's Alive to You

I was 12 when The Unimaginable happened. The thing that parents carry as one of their worst fears -- and kids have no idea that they should even need to be afraid of.

We were already in the new town under duress: The big house that my family had built in the mountain estates was too much for the downward turn in the economy, so it sold for a loss and we moved closer to the city -- to this ugly little rental in the town where my grandmother lived.

It was such an embarrassing and sad little house; dirty white -- not off-white or winter white, just dirty white with faded black awnings and cracks in the steps, framed by the most unstable banister that tricked you off balance when you tried to step to the front door. We should have taken that as a sign to not live there, but we didn't. It was such an eyesore compared to the home where we had just been. My middle sister and I gathered all of our spare change to buy flowers to plant in the awkwardly empty planter. It was as if it was embarrassed too -- and sadly, our efforts only made it seem like the planter, and we, were trying too hard. The word best to describe it was "pitiful."

Months went by and I lived in this little wreck of a home, in a wreck of emotions, hiding in my bedroom that overlooked our neighbor's field -- where the monsters lived who did The Unimaginable to me for months. I lived with my new secret -- of the bad thing that happened and kept happening, while my parents were too busy fighting over finances and frustrations to really notice that I was crumbling inside. My religious faith was of the "sit, kneel, and stand" variety -- which I cherished, and which normally comforted me, but despite my deep need for comfort, was failing miserably.

Until a new group of people visited our parish. It was a revival of sorts, where "the power of the Holy Spirit" was the focus, and cool, upbeat music was the new way to sing praise. The solemn service continued upstairs, while the church basement came alive with clapping along to freedom songs, and prayers that were spontaneous and honest. I felt like my soul was starting to mend... my secret was safe with God, and I stopped feeling so very broken and alone.

It was the music that truly touched me, and a certain musician in particular. His name was Keith Green -- a gritty skeptic who had turned "grateful" -- complete with a Jesus beard and a poet's heart. His life had been transformed by this man, "Jesus," and Keith couldn't stop writing about it. Not just the songs that touched you deeply, but the funny ones and the truth-telling ones. He made me laugh and smile. He made me feel like I knew him.

So much so, that I promised to myself, "One day, I will meet him -- and we will be friends."

Until the music was interrupted one day on the Christian radio station, and the host announced that Keith Green had just tragically died in a plane accident.

I was devastated.

He had been a lifeline to my healing, and I never got to tell him -- and we never got to be friends.

When my tears ran out and I could find words again, I made a new promise to myself: "One day, I will meet his wife -- and we will be friends."

That was the summer of 1982, when I was 13 years-old.

I had just finished recording a CD project to benefit the people in South Sudan in the Spring of 2001.

My life became my poems, and my poems became my songs. My career in music -- as a pianist, vocalist, and songwriter, had given me the most amazing opportunities.

I had started writing my own songs after my spiritual awakening. The Unimaginable had led me to the church basement, which led me to experience Jesus, which led me to Keith's music, which led me to my own. I had a lot to say after I went through so much healing.

I gravitated toward the music of other reflective contemporaries like Carly Simon, Billy Joel, Jackson Browne, and Carole King. But my love was diverse, and I was also drawn by another time period -- the stylings of Cole Porter and Billie Holliday, and the many standard artists of that time. Passion and confidence -- and my parent's beliefs in my gifts -- led me to a professional career at a young age, performing at country clubs and hotels when I was just 15. I felt that I fit in better with the 40 and 50 year-olds, who were putting tips in my jar and offering to buy me drinks, than I did with my peers who hadn't lived as much life as I had by that time.

Now here I was, 32 years-old, singing and sharing my music and stories -- this time, in front of a room of 500 people, mostly African Americans, who were excited for our project for Sudan.

At the end of the applause and the amens, I walked off the stage to the courtyard where I could take a deep breath and shake out the extra energy I was holding.

A woman with my fair coloring and a matching bump on her nose, came up to me and hugged me tightly. She pulled back and looked me in the eyes, "Are you Jewish?" she asked.

I shook my head, "No" and smiled in a curious way at this stranger who had her arms wrapped around me, "I'm Italian but I've always felt like part of me was Jewish - or wished I could be." She smiled a wide smile, revealing a slightly crooked front tooth. She tilted her head, "You can be Italian and Jewish. I bet that you are." She moved her hands to my shoulders and squeezed them with conviction, "That song. That message. Wow. The Holy Spirit is all over you. You're on fire, lady, you really are." She said as she stepped back.

I put my hand out to greet her, since we had already hugged and talked nationality and all, "I'm Stacey Robbins. Nice to meet you."

She put her hand in mine and it felt like electricity. "Nice to meet you, Stacey Robbins. I'm Melody Green."

———

It seemed like a fast friendship, but she had been in my heart for 20 years. Her husband was woven into the fabric of my inspiration -- for my spirituality and my career -- and now she was part of my life. Melody invited me to stay with her in her home in Kansas, where I sat at Keith's piano with the infamous picture of his silhouette behind me.

"I don't know what to do, Mel." I turned to where she was sitting, where we had been having deep, bonding conversations, and said, "I feel like I'm ready to transition out of music, and into speaking to women more -- I really want to help them get through the gnarly stuff that made them feel like a victim, and help them to find who they are again. To let them know that they're not what happened to them -- that they're not broken -- that that's a lie..." All of those things I had personally experienced, but hadn't yet shared with Mel.

"...but I'm so identified with this part of my life as a musician, that I don't know if anyone will let me be something new."

She looked intently at me -- listening not just to my words but to the Spirit she believed in, and shook her head. "Stacey, I went through this, too, about 15 years after Keith died. I want you to know this: It's not anyone's responsibility to 'let you' be anything. It's up to you. It's your responsibility." She glanced down for a second and closed her eyes. She lifted her head again and spoke to my soul,

"You need to do what's 'alive' to you."

"Do what's alive to you, Stacey."

Those words both haunted me and beckoned me -- not just back then, as I went through that career change from full-time musician to being a speaker and writer -- but as I followed other desires over the years that others would not fully understand:

- Raising my kids without a TV
- Living our 'Indoor Camping Experiment' with a low-electricity household
- Giving up our rental and taking the kids across the US and to Europe for 6 months instead of keeping them in school

And on and on and on...

We just did unconventional things.

In many ways, because that's what was alive to us.

Sometimes venturing into those new areas was natural and filled with confidence - like sliding down the sweet spot of the slide at the park. A whole lot of "Wheeeeee!" and a happy landing in the sand.

And sometimes those shifts were full of doubt and effort -- like when your butt gets stuck on the side of the slide and you bump and skid your way down to the bottom with your underwear wedged up your ass. You get to where you want to be, but it's definitely not a fun trip.

I realize, looking back, that the times when it was most natural -- when things moved smoothly and quickly into a new dream was when I really, truly felt like the dream was already mine. I saw myself doing it and living it and the rest were just details, effort, and time. My heart, mind and body were all synced together and I was filled with excitement! The energy that was fueling my vision was full of happiness -- that high-vibe kind of "I'm so excited about it!!" just like a kid is excited about Christmas coming. Kids don't worry or wonder if Christmas will come. They just have confidence that the day is approaching when all the gifts will be under the tree -- and all they have to do is feel good about it and, as my Aussie friends are known to say: "Have a few more sleeps in between."

I've felt that clear kind of excitement at different points in my life and it's been powerful.

One of those clear and easy times that stands out: I was dreaming about creating an app for my Bloom Beautiful book. Bloom Beautiful is one of those yummy gift books you give your girlfriend or yourself, full of inspirational quotes that make you just feel good about being you. I penned the quotes after having a disastrous three years of working on a book that I never released because I felt like I had lost my voice. Bloom Beautiful was my collection of bite-sized wisdoms where I could find my voice again. So, it was more than a "book of quotes" -- it was a return back to me and to trusting my heart. To add to the healing of my soul, my dear friend and amazing graphic artist, Susannah Parrish, did all the playful and whimsical art. It was such a soul-lifting project, and because of that I wanted there to be an app based on the book, so that people around the world could just wake up to inspiration and carry it with them all day long.

I had that "Christmas is coming" kind of anticipation about the app even though there was nothing on the table but my desire. There was no doubt. No worry. No wringing of my hands or mental torments of "Am I worthy enough to have this??" going on.

Nope.
Just pure, little kid, Christmas excitement.

I dreamed, and thought about it, and talked to my good friend, Dave, for about 2 weeks. He helped me brainstorm, and I did research and got quotes on how much it would cost. Even though I didn't even have 2 extra pennies for this project, I was going to make it happen -- there was no doubt, even though I had never done this before.

Then one day, a few weeks into the conversation, I was driving my family for a little visit to the cousins in Arizona. We were on the seemingly endless, mind-numbing Route 10 from California when I got a phone call from one of my dearest friends in the world, August Brice:

"Stacey! Hal (her wonderful husband and business partner) said to me, 'We should build an app for Stacey's Bloom Beautiful book. We love it so much, it should be turned into an app for everyone to enjoy!'" Their company, HeilBrice, is all about making dreams come true with their gold-standard creativity and marketing. Even though I hadn't said a word to them about my dream, they had it, too. We were all waiting for Christmas, together!

So, on that day, the energy, excitement, and research turned into an incredible offer and partnership. And to this day, I get emails from all over, thanking me for this app as people share it all around social media.

The desire. The dream. The energy. The effect.

It's *alive*.

But there are times that we have a dream *and* we doubt. It's not a clear space. It doesn't feel like "Christmas is coming!" Nope. It feels more like we have to create a whole new freakin' holiday and get buy-in from everybody -- and half of the "everybodys" are rolling their eyes at us.

That's the part that I brought to Mel that day when she gave me that advice: The not-clear space in me. We all have those times, where dreams and doubts collide.

It makes me think of some of the old Bible stories I remember from growing up. There was one where Moses was leading his people, the Hebrews, to a place God had directed, and they needed to cross the Red Sea. Only one problem: Their enemies were close behind them.

Okay, two problems:

The Hebrews ran straight toward the water

With their enemies close behind them.

They couldn't go anywhere without risking their lives. To turn back or to head into the waters -- both were certain death. They needed a miracle in order survive. God instructed Moses to lift his shepherd's staff. Moses did as he was commanded, and as he did that, the seas parted -- and the scripture says that his people "walked on dry ground" to the other side.

Seas parting. Dry ground.

Cool.

Easy.

But then, there's another story -- about a dude named Joshua who took over as leader after Moses died. Joshua was promised by God to have a certain land -- only he had a problem, too: The Promised Land was on the other side of the Jordan River. As if that wasn't enough of a challenge, it was flood season, so the river was wider, and the water was deeper than it normally was.

Good times.

Many had been there for the Red Seas parting, and maybe they were thinking, "Surely God will do the same thing in the same way. We'll all hang out here on the water's edge until God does his fancy 'part the seas' trick." But no. Instead of waiting for the waters to part, Joshua was instructed to have the priests walk into the Jordan River with the Ark of the Covenant overhead.

As soon as the priests stepped in, the water stopped flowing from another part of the river -- but the water didn't disappear -- it just stopped flowing. Imagine a full sink. You turn the water off -- sink's still full. The priests kept walking into the river, faithfully trudging through. The water was high and the priests were getting in pretty deep.

I picture these holy men, practically up to their nose in the sea, with little muttering bubbles rising up with these words, "Great, thanks for stopping the extra water, but ummm... I'm floating here, God. I only have so much strength to make it across with this ark in my hands and I'm not the tallest guy in the tribe. You said you'd make us walk on dry ground. You've probably noticed -- this isn't so dry..." (Okay, those would be my little rants with the Divine. At which point, you'd probably read about the ground opening up and swallowing me, whole.)

The next part of the text says that the priests got to the *middle* of the river and "stood on dry ground."

It took them until they were in the middle. After carrying a heavy ark -- the sacred thing -- into deep waters.

After expecting it would be easy, like the last time.

The dream and the miracle -- it took time.
And some effort.
And a lot of faith.
And something different than they expected.

Sometimes, the seas part and it's clear to see that the promise is ours to have -- and sometimes, we have to take these big faith steps into the middle of the deep waters before the miracles, that support our dreams, come about.

The first way is my favorite -- because, you know, it's easy and it feels good.

I like "easy" and "feels good." Who wouldn't?

The second way teaches me, stretches me and grows me. The second way bonds me to the experience, the people and God -- in the same way that the pain of childbirth bonds you and your baby. It strengthens me and reminds me what Glennon Doyle Melton lovingly reminds us, "We can do hard things."

Which is good, because, sometimes we have to, in order to fulfill our destiny and give birth to our dreams.

But we don't want to do hard, just for the sake of doing hard. I know too much for that to be appealing after nearly five decades on terra firma.

What makes the hard worth it, is doing what makes you feel connected to your truest, deepest, highest self.

What makes you feel free and unafraid of life?

What makes you feel like you're living your purpose and who you're here to be?

What makes you feel *alive*...

It's not about doing the things that other people expect you to -- because that always requires other people's approval in order for you to feel good and whole -- and you're not here to run your life by committee.

It's about being able to do what feels good
(While doing no harm)

Doing what feels whole.
What feels true.

So, what is it for you?

Whether it's come to you with Pure Inspiration,
Or on the heels of The Unimaginable.

Whether it's after witnessing a miracle,
Or walking into deep waters.

Whether it's sliding down the sweet part of the slide
Or having your underwear wedged up your butt...

What is it
That feels like Christmas
And feels like it's worth it?

Whatever that thing is?
That's your soul's heartbeat.

And when you lean in closer and feel it pulse in a way that brings you joy, no matter the cost,

That's how you know what's alive to you.

6
Living in the Land of Not-Knowing

Angela and I were in Florence together.

A Best-Friend, Dream-Trip Come True.

Well, sorta.

It was a Running To/Running Away kind of trip. Running To was obvious: It's Italy. You can drink the best cappuccino by morning, drink the best glass of chianti by night -- and in between eat the best gelato all. day. long.

The Running Away bit was that each of us had just gone through a time that would go down in the annals of our lives as:

"A Year We Would Most Like to Forget."

After Angela's divorce, her teens were giving her a run for her money -- and her soul. Split loyalties and upside-down hormones don't make things calmer in a family crisis. In the middle of all the upset of ending a marriage, Angela's father died -- the patriarch of the family and the family business -- and it just pulled the rest of the rug out from under her when she was barely standing already. It grips at a momma's heart to have to be everything for your kids, when you feel like you're barely half of you,

for you.

My year left me feeling thrust out of Life As I Knew It and tossed into the Great Unknown: the kids and the bullying thing, the condo rental skyrocketing and throwing us out of our market, which incidentally was announced the month *after* my husband lost his job -- and the month *before* my youngest got injured in a soccer game, landing him in a wheelchair.

We might need more than one cone of gelato or one glass of wine.

We may need a vat.

Of each.

Per day.

Angela and I had been at this whole best-friend-thing for about 34 years. She's absolutely adorable with her tiny, Italian curvy frame, and long, curly hair (her dad called her "Pastenie" which means "Little Pasta"). Her contagious smile and infectious laugh made you feel like she knew a secret that would make you happy to know, too. Angela's beauty has an ease to it and her style, a class.

I remember when she was teaching her daughter to be sure that if the dress was shorter and showing more leg, you made sure your top was covered. "It's not lady-like to let it all hang out in every direction." As her daughter would say back, "Yeah. No one needs to see all of that."

Which, incidentally, she also informed me of one day when I tried to go to the Farmer's Market without a bra. I promptly went back into my room and put on a bra like every good 47 year-old should when a 16 year-old schools her.

Angela's jewelry was always the most tasteful, and genuine -- and she would never be caught dead wearing a fake Coach bag on her shoulder. It's not that she's pretentious, because she's not one bit, it's that she likes quality -- which is why I feel extra glad that she chose me as her friend.

We'd met in our first year at Bayley Ellard -- a private high school on a gorgeous campus with converted mansions as our school rooms. Angela and I shared Literature, Spanish, and a few other classes together.

I can honestly say that traveling together was a much better experience than hanging out at her house when we were Freshmen in highschool; because for all of her beauty, fun and lady-likeness, Angela has a bit of prankster in her. She'd invite a bunch of us over to the upstairs apartment in her big house on Summit Avenue. And then, try to scare the Bejesus out of our friends and me -- leading us down the dark stairwell that smelled of formaldehyde -- because it led to the dead bodies in the basement of the funeral home that her family ran.

So, because I'm not an idiot, I much prefer Florence over a dark basement with Angela.

This trip was part celebration of our friendship, and part Thelma and Louise moment, escaping from the insanity of our lives.

We were going to have so much fun. We left the bulk of our emotional baggage in the US, and while I usually over-pack, this time I had packed lightly. The truth is that I'm just tired of holding so much in life. My closet looks like my car, my car looks like my purse, my purse looks like my head, and my head looks like my heart -- all filled to the brim and overburdened with stuff I put in but don't ever really take out.

All of my self-improvement pursuits were helping me over the past years to lighten up and now, my yoga training was taking it to the next level. I filled one carry-on, strolly-thing-y thing for my three outfits and pjs, with enough room in the front pocket for two items: My computer and one of my books that I wrote for women with Hashimoto's (an autoimmune dis-ease where the body attacks the thyroid). I try to always travel with a little something to give away -- to a weary mom juggling infants on the plane, or for one of my other serendipitous encounters. I usually offer a little prayer to stay in tune with who that might be. This time my prayer was, "God, please direct me to who needs this book. I wish it were in Italian -- dang, I'd love to have this translated in Italian -- hopefully this person can read English. Show me who needs this."

Right now, Angela and I were the ones in need.

So, our trip to Italy was the perfect remedy.

Our first four nights of de-stressing were in a Tuscan villa with private wine tours and cooking classes -- there's nothing a stuffed, fried zucchini flower and a good glass of white wine can't cure. After, we left the Tuscan hills and headed to the City Center of Florence. Just steps from the Duomo in an apartment with marble floors and a fresco ceiling. We were enchanted, entranced, and intoxicated.

We wanted to stop in a certain shop before dinner but found ourselves walking down one cobblestone street that looked just like the last 12 cobblestone streets we had hobbled down. Angela was flipping the map over and back and side-to-side in frustration.

Our feet were sore, our stomachs were empty, and we were lost.

We all have roles that we play. Angela and I take turns playing follow the leader. In New Jersey, she leads. In California, I lead. And almost every place else in my life, with almost everybody else, I lead.

But I had just spent 4 months living in a yoga class for my teacher training - and a lot of shit comes up on the mat. A lot of the false self gets presented, and the roles we play in order to be accepted and feel worthy, gets revealed.

I had the revelation during those classes that I still needed to learn the lesson of *partnership* and not always taking everything on my own shoulders.

I could feel Angela, with her map-flipping frustration, waiting for me to jump in and lead with the map.

So, I stood there in the face of my best friend's expectation and the big pull inside of me to meet it -- and I stepped onto my mental mat, put my hands in prayer position, and took a deep breath.

On the exhale, I heard Words with No Voice (the name I call God) say to me,

"You're not lost.
You just don't know where you are.
And that's different."

I looked up and smiled while the moon gleamed off of the Duomo in the Fall night air.

I touched my friend's shoulder and said, "We don't need this right now. It's too confusing. What do you say we just go to dinner?"

We were both relieved and I asked a passerby, "Dov'è il Centrale Mercato?" The Central Market was where we had lunch downstairs earlier that day -- a prosciutto panini for Angela, bocconcini (little mozzarella balls) and tapenade for me, and deep glasses of *vino bianco* for us both. The earthier bottom floor of the building was where the street food was sold, as well as it being the place you could buy your favorite market items: briney peppers and olives, freshly plucked chickens, perfectly aged provolone, and pretty much anything you'd need to make for an authentic culinary experience.

The upstairs in the Central Market is a completely different experience. Less earthy and rustic, more modern menus and playful art -- with a piano that invites you to sit down and share your song with the world (such a different experience than being in the US with the "please don't touch" signs that adorn most instruments). We had peeked upstairs after our lunch and decided we would eat on the second floor that night for dinner.

Angela and I picked a fun spot and were escorted to the seating area. There was nary a soul in sight as we approached the tables. I looked at my phone and realized that it was only 6:30. Too early for most Italians to eat dinner as they were sitting below having aperitivo until 7. But we were hungry before we started our adventure 90 minutes ago and were really famished now.

"We'll take that table." I pointed to the best two seats overlooking the market. Our server shook his head, "Mi scusi. Those seats are taken."

I scanned my eyes around the completely empty restaurant and said, "Okaayyy. Um, how about those two?"

And picked the two right next to the two best seats.

He nodded. We were good.

I smiled at how odd it seemed but then this thought came to me, "We need to meet the people who are going to be sitting here."

We sipped wine and kept saying things to each other like, "Oh my god. Can you believe we're in Italy?" and "Would you look at the light fixtures? They're a work of art!" when two handsome, well-dressed gentlemen sat beside us.

They were talking with passionate hands and big smiles and laughs. Angela saw me staring and kicked me under the table.

"Ow! Why did you do that?" I scrunched my nose at her while I rubbed my leg, the spot where the future bruise would be.

"Don't start..." She said pointing her head toward them.

Angela knows me and knows that I don't hit on men. What she does know is that we always have the most amazing, unbelievable encounters together -- mostly because I engage people when sometimes she wants to stay shy and quiet.

"Ange," I leaned forward and whispered, "I'm supposed to talk to them. I think I have something *that* one needs." I pointed to the dark haired man in the expensive, well-tailored suit.

She rolled her eyes and took a big gulp of wine.

"Okay. Here we go…" She said in her best Ethel talking to Lucy kind of way.

And off I went.

I started looking for an entry point, not able to shake how the one with the dark hair really was the one I was supposed to connect with.

I finally asked his dinner mate, what kind of drink he had just ordered. It looked like a big herb sticking out of a tumbler with ice and liquor. I had never seen that before.

"It's a rosemary gin and tonic -- they are my favorite -- may I get one for you and your friend?"

Angela kicked me under the table again. I was gonna slap her when we got back to the apartment later on.

"No grazie." I smiled to the man and turned to give the wide-eyed, "Stop that!" look to my friend.

And the conversation opened up -- of where are we from and what do we do. The man to my right was so chatty and fun -- a bicycle shop owner named Philippe who had toured with his bike all over the world. He ran other businesses, as well, and was rich with stories of amazing encounters. The other man, was quieter. Less engaged. Less wanting to have anything to do with us until Philippe asked what I did. I handed him my card. He flipped it over where there's a picture of one of my books. He started speaking in Italian to the dark-haired man. Philippe's friend looked up and started asking me skeptical questions. Still reserved, still guarded but now communicating more.

The conversation warmed to the point that, a bottle of wine appeared for us, and a plate of exquisite cheese for us all to share. The server looked confused as to where to place it, so, Philippe moved the tables together, so now we were all one.

Angela kept taking long pulls of red wine while I kept assuring her that we were okay. They knew we were married and committed. Our connection wasn't about that at all. It was playful and fun -- celebrating life and connection the way that Italians are the experts at -- and then there was this extra thing with the dark-haired man, named Delfino, who I was supposed to meet.

I could feel Angela's concern. I guess Philippe could feel it too because he said to Angela, "I wanna you to know -- we're not paying for your dinner -- we just want to share these parts of ours with you." Her shoulders relaxed and she stopped looking at the Exit sign, plotting our escape.

At one point, Philippe left to go out for a cigarette and Defino finally said to me, "My mother -- she has what you wrote about in your book." He pointed to my card.

"She has Hashimoto's?" I asked.

"Sì…" He nodded soberly.

Drawing in a deep breath, I became aware of this man as a son. A son who's mom has a health condition. Like my sons back home, who have me, a mom with a health condition. I was able to feel what it must be like to feel helpless when someone you love is struggling. I leaned in and looking at his eyes that were still not fully engaged and said, "She's an amazing woman isn't she? I bet she is strong and so devoted to you -- and I bet she works harder than anyone you know. And I bet she doesn't take care of herself like you want her to -- and that you're worried about her."

His eyes looked straight into mine and all the walls fell, "Yes. Yes. Yes."

He suddenly stopped being the guarded businessman, interrupted by American tourists. He became engaged with his heart and a stranger, for the sake of someone he loved.

Delfino leaned forward, passionately sharing with me about the divorce his parents went through and how hard his mother took it. How she is one of the most phenomenal chefs at her very own prestigious restaurants. About how he is her only child and he's worried sick about her. He just wants to help her and has been wondering how.

I listened. I shared a short version of my of deep sickness and years of overworking and self-neglect, of gaining 100 pounds, and how my journey was focused not only on the physical but on *le credenze...* the beliefs we have about ourselves and our worth -- and how when I worked on that, I gained my health and lost my weight -- it helped me to get better, faster.

"I will get her your book." He was decided.

"Does she read English, Delfino?" I asked, hoping against hope.

"No. Is it translated in Italian?"

I shook my head, "No. I'm sorry."

"No problem -- I will translate it into Italian so that she can read it and she can have health, too."

I said, "I have one copy that I brought with me - I believe it was meant for your mom. I would be happy to meet with her and give it to her or, I can just drop it by your office, if you'd like."

He didn't say a word to me. He picked up his phone and made a call and started speaking in Italian to someone. He covered the bottom part of the phone and jutted his chin toward us "Are you free tomorrow night?" he asked to Angela and me. I tucked my legs under my chair so that she couldn't kick me again, "Sì... we are." I nodded in response.

He hung up and leaned forward to us again, "Tomorrow night, you will be my guests at my mother's restaurant. You can bring the book for her and talk with her there. I will have someone, a female, there to translate when you meet with my mother so that she can understand more. But first, you will be my guests."

I thanked him deeply.

"No, grazie mille, Stacey." He said with a warm smile on his face, reaching out his hand to shake mine, "Thank you."

I looked up and saw Philippe standing there talking to Angela and she was explaining what had happened and he said something to her that made her eyes go wide and she just started laughing and pointed to me while she was.

In the meantime, Delfino ordered everyone an after-dinner wine to pair with what he said was one of the best panna cotta -- we dived in and I practically had an out-of-body experience it was so delicious. I noticed how different it was from when we first came together -- the energy inside of me was peace and anticipation, but now it was peace and satisfaction.

We sat there, silently savoring, not just the creamy-dreamy sweetness of the dessert -- that I'm pretty sure the angels from heaven came down and kissed -- but of the encounter that left us all feeling like some kind of magic fairy dust and destiny had given us the gift of finding each other.

I was sitting in my living room, on that rare, quiet afternoon in the condo we'd rented for a few years, about 2 miles from the beach in Southern California. I had opened the door on our lovely, Spring day and could feel the breezes from over the water and sand, all the way to my couch and my cup of tea.

I smiled.
And sighed.

And then, heard someone sobbing. I mean, fiercely, wildly sobbing in distress in the canyon not far from my front door.

Sometimes, the homeless population camps out in the wilderness or sometimes there are teens wanting to play "I'm a Cool Guy" with a bong or some beers. Occasionally, we've had some stragglers on meth or heroin make for an exciting time, too

It's not boring and every mom cell inside of me went running to the front door to see if I could find the hysterical woman from over the fence.

I listened, and heard her getting closer.

It's not just desperate cries that I heard -- she's screaming with pissed-off swear words in between sobs.

I looked down one path and then, down another and saw her. Medium height, dark hair, a little full around the middle with a white tank, shorts, and a red hoodie tied around her waist.

And you know, a phone to her head, giving someone named "Christopher" ear blisters with her words full of acid.

"I'M LOST!!! I CAN'T FIND YOU!!! I'M SCARED!!!" were the words in between the colorful sailor phrases.

Now, you need to know: Yeah, there are trees and such lining the canyon, but it's super spacious, and there are dirt paths, lined by a string of condos all along the perimeter in her view.

This was not a Survivor Man episode in the jungles of Africa where she was alone, with only a string around her wrist, a knife and a few drops of water in her canteen.

I mean, holy crow, I was staring at her, she was that close.

If I had hopped over the fence and scooted down the little hill across the dry wash, I could have been by her side in about 3 minutes to shake some sense into her. If I never even did that, and she just turned around, she could see how close she was to civilization.

Scanning around, I tried to find poor Christopher. Ah, there he was. Tall, dark hair, white t-shirt and jeans, with a red hot phone against his head.

If I were Christopher, I would have run the other way. In fact, part of me wanted to help him.

I called out to the girl, "Hey!!! Sweetheart! Girlfriend!!! Up here… YOU! The LOST ONE WITH THE FILTHY MOUTH AND THE BAD SENSE OF DIRECTION!!"

Okay, I didn't actually say that but I really, really wanted to.

I just said the first part.

She looked up at me from where she was on the path. She was all distraught and beside herself. I smiled and waved.

Christopher saw me too. I smiled and waved to him too and whispered,

"Run, Christopher!"

But he couldn't hear me.

And I started waving them toward each other. "SWEETHEART, YOU'RE FINE! HE'S RIGHT THERE! CHRISTOPHER, GO LEFT AND AROUND THE BEND."

I was directing traffic while they were quietly listening.

When they found each other, you would have thought that Gilligan and Mary Ann had been rescued off the island.

They were two very happy campers.

Who were never really lost --

I could see them.

They just didn't know where they were.

And that's a different thing.

We make those in-between, unknowing places so wrong. We get this idea of how things should be and who they should be with -- and then, when they're not, we feel all sorts of feelings.

Like Angela in Florence. Frustrated. Map-Flipping. Hungry and Upset.

Like me when I was waiting to hear on the new apartment we were trying to rent by the beach (after a year of travel, three months in a moldy apartment and six weeks of homelessness) and I turned into a complete wreck of a bitchy, witchy woman. (Sorry, honey.)

Or like the girl in the canyon, crying, screaming, swearing, freaking-out and mad.
Because we feel lost.

Yet, there are other times when we're perfectly okay with not-knowing where we are. On a flight to Europe from LA, I do not need, or want to know where we are at every minute. In fact, it would be exhausting to my brain and the trip would probably feel longer than it already is. I surrender the need-to-know-everything to the pilots and I settle in for my ride.

Losing weight and checking the scale every few hours. It's not how the process works. Not so peaceful and it's not going to give me an accurate view of my progress.

Planting a seed and digging it up every couple of days to see how it's growing, is not going to help it grow -- it's going to slow down the process.

Raising teenagers and feeling thrown every time their hormones misfire into anger, or pimples, or a big huff and a need for time alone -- if I try chasing after them every time there's an uncomfortable emotion or expression to make sure they're okay, just because I'm uncomfortable, is going to mess with their heads and our relationship.

I don't need to know everything, every second, of every day. That anxiety I feel when I don't know what's going on, usually comes during the times when I feel vulnerable and untrusting. That's when I put a lot of pressure on the process, in between destinations.

We've all been that girl in the canyon -- freaking out when things aren't the way we wanted them to be. And in the middle of that gap of where we are, and where we think we should be - we have a choice:

We can freak out
Or we can listen.

We can stress out
Or savor the mystery.

We can feel lost
Or we can feel guided.

And remind ourselves that just because we don't know where we are
Doesn't mean we're lost.

Maybe we were just creatively, unknowingly on our way to our
Magical Encounter, that Someone Else sees and orchestrates as we
quietly listen, and move toward our destiny

With a little more wonder,
A little less fear,
And a little more trust.

7

Take the Long Way Home

I was just driving Thing 2 to basketball practice. Got in the car with my water, my tea, my computer, and my kid -- and apparently a hundred thousand thoughts in my head -- and off we went.

I started driving toward The Boys and Girls Club, but then got to wandering in my mind -- thinking about everything that was going on for the day, for the next week, and pretty much an entire lifetime.

It all included finding a new apartment (since the old one had mold) buying a new, used car (since the old, used one was groaning), violin lessons, high school options, new sneakers, and you know, whether the boys will want to learn to ski in their 20's even though we haven't taught them how to ski while they're young -- and if our decision has, in some ridiculous way, scarred them for life.

I have issues.

I know.

While I was working every single one of them out, I made a wrong turn.

I realized this just as I missed the street that would have made us early, rather than on time.

I'm slightly addicted to being early.

"Shoot. What am I doing?" I flipped my blinker on, and then had to drive an extra 5 miles because the place is on an inconvenient island near the beach and I missed one of the only main entrances (not kidding) to get to where I was going.

If only I hadn't been so in my head with a scrillion other things.
I wish I could say this is a rare occasion…

But it's not.

The moldy apartment was the "opportunity du jour." We found mold and realized, "Oh, *this* is why we have been feeling like crap the last few months." The landlord saw that there were issues in the roof and made an offer to move us to a smaller unit, *which* was the only other unit in our little complex off the golf course. It happened to be the apartment which I had originally declined when we were looking there. I was not excited to think about moving again, to a smaller place, which possibly had mold, too.

I still had boxes to unpack from the first move, for Pete's sake.

Plus, I was already challenged by sharing one bathroom with three other healthy colons. I thought, *maybe this is a sign -- and our opportunity to find something bigger off-site.* So, I made what I thought was a reasonable counter-offer, that pissed off the easy-to-piss-off landlord and complicated -- well, pretty much *everything.*

I wish I could say it's the first time I've complicated something,

But it's not.

Yeah. I've had a few key moments in my life where I've made sticky situations, a little stickier. And because the theme music for this started to sound familiar, I sat down to examine myself.

It was like that moment when you start sniffing in the air. You know that smell. It's not a good smell. It hints distinctly of dog poop and, as you turn around looking with indignation for where it's coming from, you look down at your own shoes and realize:

It's you.

Yup.

Had that moment.

It was me.

Oh don't get me wrong, the landlord was being a total ass, but for some reason, I couldn't settle on blaming him for what I needed to see in me.

With a big "Ugh!" and thousands of dollars with a possible lawsuit on the line, I sought advice from my circle of friends.

Tracy said, "This needs more male energy; let Rock handle this. I think if you use your male energy, it'll wipe you out." She knows about my adrenal glands waving little white flags, and about the thyroid flare that I was healing from.

Silvana, my chiropractor who's a kind of Hindu, kind of Buddhist, fellow Italian/East-coast girl said to me: "Get your energy out of this. Leave it to Rocky. Just be grateful. The only energy you need to spend is in gratitude."

First of all, my husband hates when I "leave it to him" on stuff like that, but I heard a distinct theme from my good friends and just got quiet, except to say, "Thanks."

So, in the space of the gratitude that night and the next morning, this revelation came to me this way:

Stacey, you sometimes make life harder than it has to be.

That was it. Nothing fancy. No special drumroll or clash of cymbals. Sometimes the truth just comes in plain simple packages left at the door of your heart. The revelation had actually been coming for a while, like a plane circling overhead, waiting its turn for clearance on the runway. Today, it landed.

Gratitude is a great space-clearer -- it gives truth a place to set itself down.

Sigh.

So, I shared the "a-ha!"moment in a text to my friend, Dave:

"Hey, do you know that I sometimes, occasionally -- rarely, actually -- make life harder than it has to be?"

He wrote back, "Yup. You do."

Which was slightly embarrassing, because it's sort of like having someone peel the "Kick Me" sign off your back. They already knew something you've just figured out. *Ouch.* But Dave followed up with an explanation that made me more curious than ashamed, "You have a worldview that's constantly looking for a lesson, Stacey, and I think that causes you a lot of angst."

I responded with a text that said:

"Hmmm ... that's an interesting insight.
I'm about to change my world view to 'looking for donuts.'"

He didn't say anything back. I think he needs a vacation from me.

I don't blame him.

I do, too.

I have to wonder how much of this comes from nature's hard-wiring or how much comes from nurture -- or lack of nurture, maybe -- which can train you to find your way in the world, in strange, sideways kinds of ways.

Some people just come into the world knowing how to do things. My oldest son came in knowing how to hold his drumsticks, matchstick style and not to pee on me when I changed his diaper. My second son came into the world knowing how to cross his legs like an English gentleman and do math problems like a champ.

I'm not sure what comes from nature or nurture in my case, but two distinct memories come to me:

The first was when I was 16 with my high school guidance counselor. I was trying to sort some teenage angst, while not telling her the full story of the abuse I had experienced. As a result of my hiding out in front of her, she had half a picture of me every time we met. In retrospect, though, she probably knew there was more going on behind the scenes.

At one point she said to me, "Stacey, you're so smart, and I see that you have this sort of 'gift' -- you make things complicated in order to make them easy for you. It's as if that's the path you've created to find your way through to the other side of something hard. It reminds me of those mazes in a puzzle book -- you twist and turn and go all around. You eventually find your way to the other side, but you take the longer way getting there."

I remember feeling kind of proud to be that complicated.

I didn't know any better then.

The other memory that came was from when I was about 27. My

best friend in New Jersey was getting married and wanted me to be in her bridal party. The only glitch was that I was living in California. Okay, that wasn't the only glitch. I was dealing with a huge amount of pain and sickness in my body from the autoimmune dis-ease that I was diagnosed with, as well as a pretty bumpy time in my fairly young marriage. One of the things that got triggered during those messy years was a fear of flying. I just felt incredibly unsafe and out-of-control when my feet weren't on solid ground. So, I proposed to my husband that we drive in our new van across the country. As professional musicians, we had the flexibility to take three weeks off to travel: A week to get there, a week to be there, and a week to return.

He wasn't excited. We had done a cross-country trip for our honeymoon seven years before. I'm not sure that the seven years were enough time to recover from all those weeks on the road with a leaking air conditioner in a small car...*with me.* Plus, it doesn't make sense to him to drive when you could just fly for a few hours and get there for the good parts of the experience.

But that's because he's really easy and just trusts. He does. It's a gift. He poops, eats, and sleeps just about anywhere, and flying doesn't push any of his fear buttons.

But not me. Both my desire and fear got together for a pow-wow and decided to make this as miserable and expensive as possible. It took a month's savings to drive 6,000 miles in three weeks time.

We sang at the wedding. It was beautiful.
We got to celebrate my friend. It was lovely.
We got to climb in the car and drive all the way back home.

What a freaking nightmare.

Fear costs us so much.
Being in our heads costs us so much.
Not trusting costs us so much.

It all made perfect sense to me at the time. I couldn't see that I was letting fear rule my life. I just thought that I was being creative then, but in hindsight, I was able to see the pricetag.

I shared this in my Self-Mastery class recently. One of the women said to me, "It was the truth revealed to you at the time -- the one you were willing to see. You fly all over the world now. You're not in that place anymore. Now you're willing to see a bigger truth. It might not be the final one but, that's okay -- just live in that one without giving yourself such a hard time. We're all growing. We're all learning. We're all realizing."

It's true.

For the far away past, or right now -- it's true.

That messy, moldy apartment turned into six weeks of homelessness . -- where my friends, Irene and Kent, graciously hosted us in between our hotel stays and throughout our house hunting. After losing so much on the apartment and spending so much in the interim -- plus the doctor's appointments and mold detoxing -- it all finally ended with a killer great apartment, a block from the beach, twice the size as the moldy one, and with TWO bathrooms for four healthy colons.

It all worked out, even though it felt like I took wrong turns along the way.

We're all traveling.

None of us are doing it perfectly.

In all fairness, my "gift" for making things harder is actually what helps me to counsel people and to be a great coach. Because people come to me with their long-ass, complicated issues like a tangled up, fine, 18 karat gold chain and I say, "Oh wow, no problem. I know what to do with this..." And I help them to get untangled. You see,

I'm an expert at complicated. I'm able to speak to them where they are and to help them find their way to a clear space with a simple truth that sets them free.

The body does the same thing, if a valve is blocked or an organ is missing, the body knows how to reroute to make the most of a different path when the ideal path isn't available, for whatever reason.

The body doesn't judge itself - it just does what needs to be done to get where it needs to go. And then, it gets there.

None of it is wasted. Not even the hard stuff. Not the messy places, and not the missed turns.

We're all traveling.

Some of us make life easier. Some of us realize that's where we need to grow.

Some people focus on donuts.

And some just keep loving us while we get lost in ourselves, and end up taking the longer way home.

8
The Power of Gratitude

I met him while I was playing guitar for a conference at his church. His name was Gary and he was my sound man. But he ended up being more than that. Oh my lord. So much more.

He moved the speakers, adjusted my mic, untangled my chord, and even tuned my guitar (which I really appreciated since I'm mostly a piano player and this whole "tune-the-strings" thing gives my brain a cramp.) When I asked where I could find some water, he had a bottle within a minute, opened it, and he put it to my lips.

I wrapped my hand around the bottle, assuring him with my eyes *I've got it from here,* because from the way things were going, I think he probably would have drunk it for me if he could. I smiled at him in a curious way,

"Gary, can I ask you something?"
He nodded an eager, "Sure!"
So I jumped in with this awkward sentence that had been buzzing in my head, "How come you're so good at ... *serving*? What's the deal?"

He closed his eyes, seeming to understand my question, (which was good because I kind of felt like a dork) and reached into his back pocket.

He pulled out a folded, yellowed paper and opened it halfway. I saw pieces of tape holding the creases together and when my eyes settled on the faded page, I was staring at a newspaper photo of a car crash.

"I was an EMT and had a scanner going in my house all the time when the call came in about a car accident on Route 74. When the dispatcher described the vehicle, my blood ran cold: I knew who it was..." He tapped his finger on the car in the picture.

"I went down to the scene and it was one of the worst I had ever seen. They had to bring out the jaws of life," he glanced up at me, "because that was the only way they could get my kids out."

Oh, Jesus.

My breath stopped as he told me more of the story with tears in his eyes. About how his three oldest kids were in the car with their friend, who was driving. Gary's 14 year-old son, his 15 year-old daughter, and his 17 year-old son -- who was just months away from graduating.

A drunk driver coming home in the morning after an all-night binge, had hit the kids head-on while they were on their way to school.

"We all got them to the hospital and after they were triaged, the doctors came out to tell me the news: My 14 year-old was in surgery to remove his spleen -- he was going to be okay. My 15 year-old daughter who was an all-star soccer player, was never going to walk again. And my 17 year-old -- who was just days away from his 18th birthday..."

He closed his eyes as the tears poured down, "And wasn't going to make it through the night."

We both stood there in grief while Gary shared what happened.

"I stood in the waiting room, Stacey. The doctor had just come out to tell me that I was going to have to go say, 'Goodbye' to my son and I just couldn't. I couldn't do it. I paced the waiting room, by myself, just yelling at God, 'It's not enough! I haven't had enough time with them. I can't say 'goodbye' when it's not enough time."

"I knew people could hear me through the glass in the waiting room, but I didn't care. My whole life felt like it was dying. I just kept pacing and crying and yelling at God when I finally took a breath -- that's when I heard God inside of me say,

'Thank me, Gary. Just thank me for the time you've had.' "

Gary stood in front of me, shaking his head.

"I couldn't. I was too angry. Too *hurt*. I told God: 'No. I'm not going to thank you for taking my babies away. What kind of sick God are you to ask me to thank you for the time when it's not enough.'"

He lifted his head toward me, his eyes determined and pleading.

"But again, I heard that voice say to me, 'Just thank me for the time you've had with them, Gary.' "

"I was so broken. I was mad. But, for some reason -- maybe it was all those Sunday mornings of hearing about God's love. I don't know ... I was willing. I just took a deep breath and imagined my youngest son in surgery and said, 'For my son, Ryan, of 14 years, thank you.' "

"I thought of my daughter -- the one who I wanted to walk down the aisle but would never walk again. I said: 'For my daughter, Natalie, and her 15 years, thank you.' "

His head dropped and tears fell on the newspaper he was holding.

"And then, my heart broke, Stacey. Thinking of my son. Of the college he would never go to, of the football games he would never play, of the fishing times and talks we would never have, I just lost it and through clenched teeth, I said, 'For my precious son, Michael -- of almost 18 years -- thank you.' "

We both stood there, sobbing. After a minute, Gary wiped his face and moved his hand toward his chest.

"The more I said thank you -- over and over again," he patted his chest in a steady rhythm, "my heart started changing. Something was changing. I can't explain it but those 'thank you's' broke even the brokenness inside my heart."

I couldn't even see Gary anymore through my tears and I had to wipe them away to watch him unfold the rest of the newspaper. There was a picture of his youngest son, smiling. "Ryan made it through just great. We have to be careful with infections and stuff since he doesn't have a spleen, but he's doing just great."

Next to the picture of his son was a picture of his daughter, Natalie -- running with a soccer ball -- I assumed it was an older picture of her but Gary shook his head, "They said she'd never walk again, Stacey. But she not only walked, she ran. All of the physical therapy and her strong determination -- and so many prayers -- she's playing soccer again. My girl is running again."

And then, he opened the last fold. I gasped and turned to Gary, searching his face for confirmation.

It was a picture of a man wearing a graduation cap. "This is Michael. They said he wouldn't live through the night, but he did. Barely. And he kept living, barely. It was touch and go for a while and he is still dealing with some effects from the swelling on his brain, but he did it.

It took him an extra year but he finished high school and graduated. And they held his spot in the college that he's starting this Fall."

We were a mess. Gary, the sopping wet newspaper, and me -- just standing there in awe with what he had just shared.

"It never would have been enough, if I hadn't said 'Thank you' in that hard moment. Nothing would have ever been enough. Not those years I had with them or the years that I still get to have. I would have lived resentful of what I lost and afraid of losing what I had left."

And then, he said the words that stilled me, "God wasn't asking me to say 'thank you' for him -- he was asking me to say 'Thank you' for me."

I needed a second to breathe that in. "God knew that I needed it in order to let them go -- because he knew I needed it so that I could have them back without always being afraid every time they left the house -- and every time that police blotter went off in my livingroom...

The thank you wasn't for him, Stacey.

The 'thank you' was for me."

I've thought of Gary, a lot, since I met him on that stage in 2000 in State College, PA.

I thought of him when my first son was 18 months old, lying in a hospital bed, wires all sticking out of him because of some unknown infection, unconscious, and not coming to.

I thought of Gary when my second son was 3 years-old, lying in the same hospital his brother had, grey all over his face and body because the hole in his heart was trying to make itself known.

I will never pretend to understand the magnitude of Gary's horrific experience, but I have taken the template of his lesson with me. The lesson of gratitude in the face of the unspeakable. I feel like it's the least we could do -- to honor the lesson of another -- especially when it cost him so much to live it.

And I also recognize that in those moments, Grace speaks to us with our own messages that we uniquely need to hear. With Caleb lying there in the hospital, I heard Words with No Voice speak to me, "Surrender your place of having to know-it-all and do this perfectly. There are people here to guide you. You're not alone." My girlfriend heard, "Be Still and Know that I Am God" when her beloved sister was dying.

I don't know if we all hear something or sense something in those darkest hours -- all I know is that Gary's experience has had a unique space in my life.

I don't just bring his experience of gratitude into my hardest moments, I try to remember them in the medium times, and the seemingly mundane times.

It is compelling to me, the shift that gratitude brought to Gary's life -- and the idea that if it can be powerful in his extreme circumstance, it can be powerful for any of us, at any time...

When we choose it,

Even when we don't feel it.

There were long years in my young marriage when I wanted to throttle my husband and started picking on his weaknesses because he had broken my trust in so many different ways.

I had gotten into a habit of being negative, and, as much as I didn't like him for doing what he did, I didn't like me for being unkind. One of the ways that I broke that habit was by finding qualities in him to be grateful for.

When I am grateful, it helps me to heal
And to be present
To let go
And to move on.

It's very functional.
It's like one of those fancy kitchen gadgets that costs $29.99 at the State Fair and does a scrillion different things.

Gratitude can help you appreciate
Your kids
Your spouse
Your job
Your body

The person who's in your life
And the person who's not.

And it's surprisingly portable.

You can take it to a park bench
A movie theatre
A diner
Or even a hospital room

Gratitude is useful anywhere
And can serve us everywhere by giving us a very different perspective
Without ever leaving the place we're standing.

It transports us to experience life in a completely different way.

Gratitude is a gift from God.

When Gary said that the thank you for was for him, it made me think...

About the value that "Thank you" has -- not just to the one receiving it, but to the one giving it.

That it does something for us, that God knows and maybe why there is so much "Be thankful" in the spiritual messages we hear in the different religious texts.

What does being grateful do for us?

It slows us down
Makes us present
And feel like whatever it is that we think is not enough
Is suddenly
Enough.

We struggle with that, here in the West.

Probably one of the biggest struggles, we in First World countries face is the daily woe of "My life is such a 'good' life -- but, how come I'm not happy?"

We focus on what we feel is not enough, instead of what we have.

It's where we all walk at some point in our lives --
So close to the very thing we want
But not really enjoying it
Because we're not really experiencing it.

And because we're not experiencing it, we're not really *living*.

Experience is where life is.

Fear of Not-Enough or Not Good Enough steals the experience.

It steals our peace, our joy -- our presence to the goodness right in front of us.
The person right in front of us.

It takes us away and holds us hostage.
It blackmails us and makes us pay with the currency of "right now" in exchange for another time that is going to be *more* and *better*.

But no matter how much we sacrifice today to pursue whatever "more" we think is the answer,

it's never enough.

But gratitude -- well, gratitude changes everything.

It shifts us out of our head-spinning, hamster-wheel-running, unblinking madness and transports us into this spacious, glorious, expansive, moment where we feel truly alive -- even in the midst of our pain.

Everything changed for Gary before it changed anywhere else.

His thank you changed his heart,
And his changed heart
Changed his experience
Of the experience.

It's the same for us.

Because being grateful makes us present --
And our presence is our power.

It can make a meager portion, a feast
A lonely time, a sanctuary
A good-bye moment, a new "hello."

It's how powerful we are. And God knows it.

That's why he asks us to say "Thank you"
Because it makes us present
And that makes us powerful.

God knows we forget. Sometimes we live like the driver whose eyes wander to the side of the road -- his hands will eventually turn the wheel toward where he's looking, and the car will start to drift.

When we fix our gaze on "not enough" our whole life ends up there, In the deep ravine of

Not enough.

We see "not enough" -- and by God, with all that Divine Power in us, that's what we get.

In buckets
And droves
And silos.

A disastrous amount of "Not Enough" takes over our lives.

But gratitude shifts everything.

Gratitude focuses us and gives us eyes that see the abundance -- the enough-ness -- of right now. And when we keep our eyes, heart, and mind on all that we have, we keep having more of that.

That's why Gary was so great at serving. Because his gratitude kept him present to the right now and in the right now, he had more than enough.

From that great place of holy enough-ness, he couldn't help but give.

Gary was right:
We don't say "thank you" because God needs to hear it…

He reminds us to say "thank you"
Because *we* do.

9
The Indoor Camping Experiment

The reason my husband looks at me like he's Ricky and I'm Lucy is because I say things like this:

"Hey honey. Why don't we turn all the breakers off in the house and see what it's like to live without electricity for a while?"

His answer, "Because having electricity is called 'progress' and I like to think of us enjoying the benefits of that, you know -- with hot and cold running water, refrigerated foods, and clean laundry just a few spin cycles away."

Hmmm...he had a good point. I was suggesting the changes to help with my health condition, but I didn't want us to turn into Ma and Pa Ingalls, either.

"Okay, how about we turn off all of the breakers except for the fridge, dishwasher, and washer and dryer?"

He just stared at me.

I took it as my cue to talk more.

"Remember when we went camping for the field trip with the kids..." I started.

He interrupted, "And the inflatable mattress deflated and we were sleeping on the cold ground WHICH wasn't supposed be that cold, remember? It was only supposed to go down to 55 that night, but it ended up being 35 and we were all freezing and *you* wouldn't pee in the outhouse so I had to keep escorting you to the car to pee in the port-a-potty you brought but didn't want to have in the tent..."

I don't know why he always remembers the unflattering things about an experience. Plus, I didn't think it was really fair to blame the temperature changes on me.

I interrupted him before it got worse, "I rehearsed this as a solo." I said.

He rolled his eyes while I continued,

"ANYway, so, remember how I wasn't as dizzy when we woke up that morning?"

He nodded a slow "Yes." in my direction.

"Well, my friend, Wendy, has a really fancy device that turns off her bedroom breakers at night so that the kids can sleep without the buzz of electricity going through the house, and I thought that would be something we could do, too. Since we don't have one of those special switches, what if we just turned off the breakers ourselves to see if it helped my health?"

I had been chatting with him the prior months about how my body seemed to flip out when we went into a Big Box Store, with all of the electronics emitting the EMF's (electromagnetic frequencies).

My body seemed to do better with having my feet in the earth or at the beach -- which the scientist and woo-woo folks both called "Earthing" or "Grounding".

He sighed and agreed, kinda like he did when I asked him 5 years into our marriage if we could take the TV out of the house as a way to heal our marriage from some issues we were working on. He'd run to the television as a distraction instead of dealing with the marriage

-- which made all my Scorpio, crazy-Italian come out to play. I know we got married young, but I didn't want to live with a teenager.

He agreed to a month.

That was 20 years ago and we still don't have a TV in our house.

His superpower is Flexibility. His Kryptonite is me. He'd give me the moon if I asked for it, without a thought for himself. That's why I'm careful about what I ask for. I don't ask for diamonds or pearls or a big home or a new car. I'd rather have more time with him and less dollars in the bank or new clothes on my back. I ask for breakers off and no TV and crazy stuff like that.

He probably wishes I'd ask for diamonds.

So, we sat the boys down to share my latest inspiration.

I clasped my hands together in a "I've got a crazy fun idea for you!" kind of way,

"Hey guys! What do you think about us doing a little experiment to help mom's health? We're going to turn off the electricity in the house -- well, most of it anyway -- for a whole month and see what it's like to enjoy the daytime like we normally do, but during the night we will light candles and have a more peaceful time like we do when we're out in nature -- like that time when we went camping."

"Are we going to make s'mores and light a big fire in our living room?" seven year-old Seth asked.

His big brother, who had two years of wisdom on him said, "That would light the place on fire, Seffers. Then all our Legos would melt and we would die."

So comforting to know that he was concerned about his Legos first.

105

"Oh." His little brother seemed disappointed but then, I jumped in,

"Well, we can make s'mores in the fireplace if we want, sure...but how about we finish our experiment and then, we take a trip to the Redwoods to see the REALLY BIG TREES -- trees so big you can drive a *car* through them!"

I stretched my hands out high and wide, "Then, we'd visit our friends, Lance and Lyndia, in Santa Cruz as a way to celebrate the end of our Indoor Camping Experiment?"

The boys cheered.

Rocky looked at me with that, "I-thought-we-could-end-the-experiment-with-a-spa-that-has-electricity" kind of look.

I ignored him a little and cheered with the boys.

"Hooray!!"

We grabbed a big basket and collected a bunch of candles from my candle closet.

Okay, side note: Yes. I have a candle closet. More like a closet shelf or two, but since it's such a predominant feature, we call it "The Candle Closet".

I know that sounds crazy, after the whole "Don't want diamonds, don't need pearls" bit, but I went through a season where I had sort of a teeny, tiny addiction to candles. We'd go to a store and I'd head right for the shelf that housed every form of flammable wax I could find.

Rock would say, "We have 14,000 of these things in our closet that we never use. You're like a candle hoarder. Please -- enough with the candles!"

I'd say back, "It's more like 30 (okay, maybe 40) and not 14,000, just to be accurate. But we live in California! You never know when we're going to have an earthquake and no electricity. Plus it's so pretty that I can keep it as a "just-in-case" gift if someone drops by and…"

"And what?" He took the jar out of my hand, looked at it and then, back at me, "And needs an emergency Coconut Breeze scent wafting through their house on the day the Big One strikes?"

He rolled his eyes at me.

He does that a lot.

I took it out of his hands, "No! In case they drop by with a gift for us -- or if they're sad and need cheer. And beside, if they *did* use this during an earthquake, I'm sure it would take the edge off a little bit."

"That's a lot of pressure to put on one little candle in the middle of mass destruction."

He thinks he's so smart, but I'm the one who walked out of the store with the candle and now have a closetful just in time for our Indoor Camping Experiment so, who's laughing now…

The boys and I ceremoniously walked around the house with our full basket and placed candles and matches in different rooms -- giving the boys clear instructions on who was allowed to light (Mom and Dad) and who was allowed to blow them out (Caleb and Seth).

While we did that, Rock flipped the breakers on and off until he found the only two we needed to kick off our big adventure.

We lit the candles, and made dinner as the sun was setting -- and before we knew it, we were having the first night of our Indoor Camping Experiment.

———————

Everything was bliss: Couch snuggles, candle light and, the sounds of Charlie the Cricket singing his night time songs. *(We named every cricket we ever heard, "Charlie" -- it made us feel like we had a pet that lived forever instead of just three, little, song-filled weeks.)*

Everything was charming and right out of a modern Norman Rockwell painting until I got up to go to the bathroom and stepped on a Lego creation. I hopped and swore my way through the long, dark hallway to the bathroom, where I sat down in pain and nearly lit myself on fire.

Because that candle that looked so charming on the back of the toilet, flickering in the night, singed the ends my hair while I was trying to poop.

Lighting yourself on fire isn't very relaxing for the elimination process.

We found out that some of this "being healthier" stuff wasn't as peaceful as I had imagined and we had to really think through our days differently. The life lessons came quickly...

- Pick up *all* the Legos during the daytime when you can see them so that mom doesn't teach you a whole new set of vocabulary words when she puts you to bed.

- Cooking by candle light can seem romantic but you have to be careful to not give your family salmonella when you can't tell if the food is cooked enough.

- Christmas scented candles and summer scented candles can make for some gaggifying combinations if you're not careful.

- There's a space between sun setting and mind-quieting that can result in some boredom and temper tantrums from both the parents and the kids.

- It's important to think through the timing and what temperature your house is gonna get. In all of my enthusiasm, I forgot that it was August.

No fans.
No air conditioners.
No nothing.

Whoops.

Rock would come home after working in an air-conditioned office all day and felt like he was stepping into an oven. "What the heck? It's 86 degrees in here! Aren't you melting?"

The truth was: No, you adjust.

Our bodies were transitioning smoothly from the cool mornings to the mild early afternoons to the hot, late afternoons, into the dusk.

Our inner thermostats were adjusting.

We found our rhythms shifting, too. We moved around a lot in the morning, went outside in the early afternoons and rested a bunch in the late afternoons. We started doing what needed more light (coloring, painting, legos and reading) during the brighter parts of the day, and what we could do when we needed less (hugging, singing, sharing stories, jokes and tongue-twisters, great games of outdoor basketball and s'mores).

We naturally faded from light to dark, and noisy to quiet, from energy to stillness.

Our family began flowing with the natural pace of the days and started seeing that there was a whole other character to the 24 cycle, with a personality all its own: We let ourselves be introduced to

The Night.

We don't ever really get to know the night in our 21st Century, modern culture. The minute it gets dark, we flip on the lights, open the laptops, and turn on the TV.

Maybe it's that we're afraid of the dark or trying to be efficient to use the time to work more -- or maybe we're just unconscious of its benefits so we don't really allow ourselves to explore or savor it.

I think I've avoided nighttime and darkness -- in the way that I've avoided sadness and grief and thoughts of death.

Because it just felt like too much -- like it would swallow me whole, if I let it. I didn't want to give an inch to something that I was afraid would take a mile.

It wasn't always that way. When I was a kid, I dug deep into the cavern of emotions -- finding the most gut-wrenching poems, stories, and ABC Afterschool Specials to sink the teeth of my soul into...

...but something changed.

I'm not sure if it was the message I got from my parents -- and then, after I married, my husband -- to 'not be sad or mad', except for certain, pre-approved times and reasons.

Or if it was just that I had experienced a ridiculous amount of trauma between the time of the Afterschool Specials and adulthood.
Or maybe listening to all of the sadness that my clients would share in our counseling sessions.

Or perhaps it was this inkling that if I gave my heart over to those dark places -- that I would fall into a deep, black hole and never return.

At the risk of sounding completely woo-woo -- I deal with some of the challenges of being empathic: absorbing so much energy and so many feelings from around me that it all feels like so much: Whether it's the Kleenex or heart-tugging State Farm commercials or even Disney -- where the adventure usually begins for the main character when a parent dies -- sometimes, I just can't get past the grief to allow myself to adventure.

Maybe, at some point, I just got filled to emotional capacity.

I remember one of my guidance counselors told me in high school, "I don't know how you're going to survive in this world, Stacey. Your antennae are out there so far and you feel *everything*."

I felt proud in the moment because it felt "special", but eventually I felt shame -- like I shouldn't feel so much because others don't. I used the spectrum of other people's emotions to judge my own.

I also started seeing that I was powerful to make things happen in my life based on what I was focused on. A magician and manifester of sorts. Like when you look at the side of the road and start to unconsciously veer off in that direction, I was scared to indulge in thoughts of death or grief because I didn't want to bring more of that into my life.

And, for all of those crazy, heavy reasons, there was a practical/ optimistic/stoic part of me that felt like grief was a waste of time. If a part of me knows that "all is well" and that we're going to eventually feel better and see things more clearly then, why spend the energy there in the grief?

To which my husband would say to me, "Even Jesus wailed outside of Lazarus' tomb after he died -- and Jesus had the power to raise him from the dead."

King Solomon said "There is a time to mourn and a time to dance."

The daytime feels like dancing to me. The nighttime has had an element of mourning to me. It feels vulnerable to me and scary -- reminding me of how I struggle to trust the unknown.

I have a feeling that I'm not the only one who deals with that.

Maybe that's why the minute the sun starts to set on the outside, we make it artificially brighter on the inside and drag out the day longer while we cut off the night.

But when we do that, we avoid a really essential and designed part of our existence:

The darkness.

Here's the thing that most folks who camp, or live in the rural midwest, or live off-grid know:

The nighttime -- after you spend a little time getting to know it, is multi-faceted. It's like that quirky relative that everyone avoids talking to at the family reunions, but when you sit down and really spend time with them, you realize they are so much more interesting than you could have imagined.

And nighttime is also like the shamanic healer that makes sounds in the mysterious ceremony that you can't really understand -- and yet, you leave his presence more healed, happy, peaceful and whole, even though you don't really know what he did to get you there.

And it's like the person who doesn't talk but just sits beside you silently. Which is super comforting if they're your friend -- but super unnerving if they are a stranger and you don't know if you can trust them. I had no idea how rich the night time was until I allowed myself to get to know it.

Our little, weird indoor camping experiment drew us into the magic of night. A time when our sight decreased and our other senses kicked in -- it required something of us:

That we listen more closely
That we move more slowly
And more thoughtfully
That we rest.
That we trust.

And that we receive those inexplicable gifts that the night uniquely gives...

When you're quiet, you can hear that the nighttime sings a different melody than daytime does.

I seriously think that the stars have their own song.

You can also hear the noise better and discern where it's coming from. When our home was filled with so much silence at night, I was able to hear the sounds coming from the other houses -- their TVs and video games humming and rumbling and chatting incessantly.

I noticed how, when I'm still in my soul, I can better tell which thoughts are the good, loving, God-thoughts, and separate them from the noisy voices in my head that are coming from other people's opinions of me.

And there's so much beauty we miss...there are things that only bloom in nighttime: when the atmosphere changes and the day flowers start to close...that's when the moon flowers, evening primrose, night blooming jasmine, and other blossoms start to open.

They are often the white or lighter flowers. There's an odd efficiency to that -- they don't have to waste their "energy" to produce pigment -- and because of that, they become their own little garden nightlight: the moon reflects off of them with a contrasting brightness. Plus, they're incredibly fragrant to draw the odd mix of nocturnal creatures to pollinate them instead: Like bats and moths and other nighttime friends that you can't imagine would offer anything valuable to your world.

For all of our manufactured efforts to extend the day -- the night has its own built-in resourcefulness -- and it's own provision to the unseen parts of life that have needs, too.

For all the efforts to avoid our pain and grief, nighttime offers us a perspective that nothing else does.

There is something sadness and grief give us.
There are gifts that the evening bestows.

But we don't ever really know it until we let down our resistance to it.

———————

(SPOILER ALERT)

We love Pixar and when we took the boys to see the movie "Inside Out", it ended up a therapeutic experience for me. The main character is a little girl, Riley, who is living a happy life with her family. Then, she's thrown a curve: a big move to another town and another school.

So many changes.
So many challenges.
So much flux.

In her head, where the Emotional Headquarters are, she has different characters representing the main emotions that we all experience: Joy, Fear, Anger, Disgust, and Sadness.

Joy is running the show, most of the time. Pulling levers up in Riley's brain so that she has happy dreams and happy thoughts and a more positive way of seeing life. Joy is just what she sounds like: Perky, cheery, and believes anything good is possible.

And Sadness is just what she sounds like: Sad, a little grey and dreary, short, with glasses.

Whenever Riley feels her unique emotions through all the changes, that character who represents her feelings, comes to the forefront and is in control.

Riley is going through the worst parts of her move: Kids not accepting her at school, parents arguing, things not being familiar.

It is *not* a happy time.

Sadness keeps coming forward but Joy doesn't see the value in Sadness. Every time that Riley is sad, Joy tries to make Sadness go away.

And one day, Sadness runs away. The other emotions can't find her. Riley is melting down with no way to process the frustration and angst she's feeling because she doesn't have Sadness to help her through.

When Joy finally realizes how important Sadness is, Joy goes after Sadness to find her, to bring her back into the fold of the other emotions -- because Joy finally realizes that Sadness is essential. When she returns, Riley can feel and process her sadness and be known. Sadness plays a key role in bringing Riley out of her dark crisis as she reconnects to herself and her family again.

I have been that person -- feeling the ache of life and avoiding both, the ache *and* life, as a result. I didn't want to dig into the hurt because I was so focused on what it would ask of me instead of what it would give to me.

Like when my father died: I didn't want to experience the groaning pain of him leaving with so much unsaid -- and unlived -- between us.

Instead I got sick for three years, wracked with guilt and grief that showed up in other ways.

Because what we don't address has our address.

It finds us, one way or another, and makes us deal with it.

My religious beliefs at that time were of the "Faith Movement" and "Name It and Claim It" variety.

You know this style of faith: It's people walking around with a raging fever and flu, coughing up green stuff all over the place but when you ask them how they are, they say, "In Jesus' Name, I am perfectly well. I have never been better, and there is nothing wrong with me."

That's the Faith Movement.

You want a car with leather seats, and even though you don't work, won't look for a job, and have a car you don't take care of, you're still saying, "I declare, in Jesus' name, *that* white Lexus with leather seats is MINE! Thank you, Lord."

That's the Name It and Claim It.
Neither one of those allows a whole lotta room for any of those human things like sickness, sadness, or vinyl seats.

It's just filled with too much doubt.
And not enough God.

So, when they see sadness, they don't see holiness, they see sin.

That was me, for a while.

It didn't work, but God bless me for always trying to make things that don't serve me, work.

Sigh.

Even though I recovered from a lot of that unhelpful theology years ago, the movie "Inside Out" found some of those icky beliefs hiding in the recesses of my heart and mind, and brought them to the surface. How those "I shouldn't be human" feelings had affected my parenting, my kids, my pressure on my marriage and my joy in life. I had less joy because I was avoiding sadness.

I cried a lot in my aisle seat that day in Edward's Theatre over a Disney movie --

And I felt okay with that.

One of my clients is learning how to grieve at the tender age of 24. She just lost her young father and her teenage sister in the span of a short time. It was devastating.

She told me, "It all feels so pointless -- will there ever be a time when I feel like there's a reason to get up in the morning?"

The darkest part of the night -- when we are hurt, don't trust, are scared, or feel lost -- feels like it will never end.

It's hard to see the value in a dark place when all we want is to not be there anymore.

The desire to be on the other side of pain, the other side of grief
The other side of the night...

Gets met *through* the pain
Through the grief
Through the night.

It works with us
While we wrestle with it.

Until it stops being an enemy
And starts being a companion.

It's part of us -- and when we stop wishing it weren't
It begins to serve us

And heal us.

Pain calls us to breathe
Grief calls us to receive
Night calls us to listen

And we need all of those in our life.

In all the slowing down that it requires, it gives us a
ime to reflect and a time to plan -- or to let go of plans.

A time to appreciate, to repent and refocus.

Nighttime -- like sadness -- gives us a time to recalibrate ourselves
in alignment with our priorities. Because sometimes, what matters
most, is never so clear as when we can't see our hand in front of our
face.

That's where we get to when we stop resisting it and we give into it --

We finally realize...

We need the night.

My boys are good sports. They really are.

They did great with our month of Indoor Camping and yes, we did head up to the Redwoods afterwards to see our friends and explore the forests. And yes, it was amazing.

That night at the hotel, after our long walk through the woods, Seth wanted to head into the shower. I was ready to turn on the lights but the boys said, "No! Mom! We want to keep going!"

I smiled and said, "Guys, I forgot the candles."

They opened the drapes to let in the lights of Santa Cruz and the bright night sky. Seth and I made our way to the bathroom.

"You sure you're okay in here, Bud? It's really okay if you need it to be a little brighter."

My seven-year old turned to me and spoke sweetness to my heart,

"Yes, Momma. I'm happy for it to be just like this. It feels peaceful to shower by the light of the moon."

I loved that.

The boys enjoyed our time so much that they voted to keep going with only two breakers. So, we did. For four years. Flipping a few of them on when we had guests to come stay with us but for the better part of those years, we lived with day being day and night being truly night.

I shared about it when I spoke at a farm-to-table event as we all sat under the dark sky with candles lighting our way. The local newspapers heard about it and came and did a big article on us. Then, ABC news came out and did a feature. It was kind of fun to have friends text me: "You don't even have a TV to see yourself on."

We found a way, thanks to the World Wide Web.

We didn't do the Indoor Camping Experiment for attention
And we didn't do it to be cool
Or weird
Or different.

We did it to help my health -- which it did. I had less brain fog, better sleep, less depression, and more calm to my inner being.

But the truth is that our not-so-little Indoor Camping Experiment gave us so much more --

More time together
More conversations
More focus
More thoughtfulness
More interesting conversation starters with friends who tried to flip on light switches
More silence
More piano and violin playing.

It's funny how taking something out of your life
Can end up giving you

So
Much
More.

10
Send in the Clowns and Cue the Ninjas

We were more than a little weary before sitting down to play music for the wedding ceremony that Saturday morning in Laguna Beach.

The night before is when all the madness ensued. We were at a gig in some local restaurant -- Rock was setting up the gear and I was doing the heavy lifting of putting my makeup on in the ladies room, when one of my contact lenses started misbehaving. I took it out and it proceeded to do a Flying Wallendas fall to the bathroom floor.

Hunting it down on my hands and knees, with just minutes to spare before the first downbeat, I popped the contact into my right eye which immediately sent me an "OhNOYouDon't!!" signal with insta-pain fireworks in my right eye.

Which I ignored, like any young 25 year-old who had an agent booking her for a gig she would like to play again.

At the end of our performance, I scooted quickly back to the ladies room and peeled the hermetically sealed thing off my eyeball. The feeling was like fire and acid and other searing, hot painfulness. I knew I had to get to the ER.

It was 2:30 a.m. by the time the gear was loaded and we had the wedding to play in the morning at 10 a.m.

Oh my lord -- we had to move fast.

The emergency room at Hoag Hospital didn't get my "move fast memo." We walked in and it looked like a scene out of a zombie apocalypse. I didn't know what the hell was going on, but the triage nurse told us it was going to be about a 6-7 hour wait.

This was not good.
This was *very* not good.

A couple of hours after dawn, the doctor who examined me said, "Yes (you dingbat) the floor had cleaning chemicals on it, and congratulations, you scratched your cornea. Well done."

Okay, he didn't actually say all of that, but he might as well have.
I felt like a fool.

So, I was given a moratorium on contacts for 4 weeks and some numbing drops until the screeching eyeball pain wore off.

Great.

Except there was this one little snag: I had a wedding to play in about an hour and couldn't see a thing without my contacts in. The next option was my pair of regular glasses -- which I had sat on and crushed about a week before. The bridge was broken and taped together with first-aid tape and one of the arms was broken off.

Zombie apocalypse eyeglasses -- a perfect match to my ER experience but not a perfect match for the wedding I needed to play.

That wasn't going to work.

The only other pair of glasses that I had were from when I started college -- when I had apparently lost my mind about what "cool"was and picked a pair of light purple, oversized frames that had tinted lenses -- and yes,

Sparkles.

You know...so, that I could be *extra* cool.
I don't know why I had felt compelled to channel Elton John when I was 18 years-old, but apparently I did.

And since these were all I had, these were going to have to do.

Rock and I rushed to the wedding to set up my gear. We were exhausted with no sleep under our belts, but the merciful thing was that they had only hired me to play piano since a friend of theirs had wanted to sing. No double duty for me today. Get in, play, get out.

Easy-peasy.

Or you know,
not.

The wedding was outside, which under normal circumstances would have been beautiful, but it was summertime and Southern California has this phenomenon called "June gloom" where the marine layer gets really thick and the mornings are overcast until the sun burns off the layer around noon or 1 p.m.

This particular morning, it was cool, grey by the ocean and -- just for giggles -- it was windy, too.

Not just a slight breeze here or there -- no -- it was a Winnie-the-Pooh, blustery day, kind of windy.

So, there we were: Sitting outside, the wind whipping my music up at the edges (that my husband is frantically trying to hold down like a scene out of the Three Stooges) with not even a wink of sleep and with huge Elton John sparkly, purple glasses on my face and a numb, bum eyeball that could barely see what I was doing.

It was quite a look.

The vocalist sat beside me, staring in shock at our own little "hold-down-the-music" circus, and smiled weakly in our direction.

Finally, the pastor cued me to start the processionals.

I performed the carefully pre-chosen songs for the guests to be seated. Once that was done, I played the song for the mothers of the bride and groom to be escorted down.

And then, I played the song for the groomsmen to walk in.

Only one problem:

They didn't.

The groomsmen were nowhere to be found by the end of the classical piece. If I played it again, everyone would know that they missed their cue.

I looked at the other pieces left to play: Canon in D for the bridesmaids: nope. The Wedding March for the Bride: nope. Trumpet Voluntary for the recessional: nope.

I had nothing left to play for the groomsmen to walk down!

I turned to Rock and whispered for him to give me my gig bag from the night before. I reached in and grabbed the first book out of the bag, opened it to the first song in the book, and started playing.

The vocalist hummed at the pretty melody while the groomsmen began walking down the aisle with big grins. I turned to my husband for a quick thumbs up but he was vigorously shaking his head at me with his eyes really, really wide, "Nononononononononono!" kind of way.

"What?" I hissed, irritated with him, "It's a pretty song!"

I rolled my eyes under my Elton John glasses and then, it hit me:

Oh shit.
I was playing "Send in the Clowns."

That lilting melody that people love, but with the lyrics that make you think of clowns when you're supposed to be thinking of handsome, upstanding men.

I glanced up at the groomsmen, happily walking in their penguin suits, while whispers started from the guests,

"Is she playing Send in the Clowns??"
"I think she's playing Send in the Clowns..."

Giggles started in the congregation and I couldn't help myself. I'm playing my song with the wind blowing everything around, with clueless groomsmen, the whispering guests, the horrified vocalist who had stopped humming when she realized what song it was -- and me, with my shoulders bouncing up and down in silent, sleep-deprived, cornea-scratched, purple glasses laughter -- with the video camera pointing right at me.

Oh good. They've got this on video for all of time immemorial.

Perfect.

Thoughts flashed through my mind of me needing to move to another town where I could start over.

Do they have a witness protection program for people like me?

Would I ever be able to live down playing Send in the Clowns today?

Life can be so messy sometimes.

Whether it's recovering from a bonehead maneuver of not rinsing a contact lens off
or something larger.

There is something so uncontrolled about it all.

Here we are, just trying to figure out how to live the Life of Our Dreams, when something interrupts our plans in small, medium, or ginormous ways.

In retrospect, the contact lens was relatively small. Not all of the bumps in life have been that smooth.

Which my boys reminded me of one day when we were chatting. They were on the littler side -- about 8 and 6. They were declaring their pride in me about something that I did -- I think it was patience in a stressful situation (it was one of those good days that we sometimes have as parents -- before I hit perimenopause with symptoms that made my sense of humor run away from home and a broomstick seem like my most fitting form of transportation).

"Your mom and dad would've probably hit you or swore at you for doing what we did, but you were really kind to us, Mom."

I held my breath for a second wondering if my mother heard that, all the way in New Jersey, 3000 miles away.

I felt conflicted.

Grateful that my kids experienced my kindness -- But kind of cringe-y, that I had recently shared about some of the harder parts of my growing up years.

It was sad that they might think that's all my childhood was...

As if it were only the non-shiny moments of my parents, parenting. Drawing in a deep breath, I looked in their earnest eyes -- such advocates of me, and I said, "Thank you for loving me. And yes, there were times my parents were really impatient and really physical in their frustrations -- and that really was *not* great. It was not right and I didn't like it at all!" They nodded and I went on, "AND that's not all they were: They were also so funny and loving, creative and supportive. They believed in my gifts and they worked very hard to provide the things that they thought were important for my sisters and me."

Caleb, a.k.a. "Captain Justice" said, "But they hit you -- and I would beat anybody up who would hit you." He had tears of passion in his eyes and his fists clenched. Seth, his trusty sidekick, slammed the table with his hand, "And I would tie them up so Caleb could do it, too."

Oh good.

Thing 1 and Thing 2 to the rescue.

Actually, and honestly -- it felt kinda nice. Especially after not feeling very protected in my life -- these guys really spoke from the heart -- and that totally touched, and healed mine.

But there was a bigger lesson here that I wanted to share.

"Guys, I love you so much. And even though I do -- I don't do everything right, do I?" They shook their heads. They know I don't. They started sharing the list of how I burned the gluten-free monkey bread on Christmas morning, and how I was sassy and loud to Daddy sometimes, and how I accused Caleb of doing something when it was really Seth's fault.

"Oh, and remember the time you were at the Farmer's Market and you and the lady pulled out at the same time and hit bumpers and you said, 'SHIT!' " Seth looked at his big brother, "But that was okay Caleb because that was a serious situation."

Oh my god. Where's the spoon to eat them up?
So much grace. So much love.
So freakin' hilarious.

"Anyway, boys -- the thing is this: We all make mistakes. We all make choices that have tough consequences and we all blow it on something, right?"

Their heads bobbed up and down.

I took a little detour for a moment and asked them, "Who thinks it would be great to be a ninja?"

Oh my gosh, that's all I heard about for YEARS -- how they wanted to be ninjas. They both raised their hands eagerly in the air.

"What do ninjas like to do?"

"Climb!" Caleb shouted.
"Jump!" Seth yelled.

They both started doing martial arts moves in their chair, whacking each other with flailing arms.

"And where do they like to climb?" I asked them.

"ROOFTOPS!" Seth shouted at the top of his lungs.

"YES!" I cheered and we were all really excited. Then, I quickly bent low and I whispered to them as their eyes widened,

"Do the ninjas always have everything placed perfectly to climb? Is there a perfect rock and a perfect branch to get to the top of the roof?"

They both shook their heads back and forth.
"What do they have to do?"

It was quiet as they fixed their gaze on my eyes in anticipation of my answer.

"They have to use whatever is there. If the rock is really low and the branch is really high -- they just use it the best they can -- and they learn how to jump off of whatever it is that is in front of them. They become really, really, really, *really* good jumpers."

They nodded seriously, confirming I was right.

"Caleb. Seth." I looked each one in the eyes. "Life isn't always going to go exactly right. Mom will make mistakes, Dad will make mistakes, you will make mistakes. But you know what?"

They watched my face, waiting,

"You can use ALL of that. The good stuff AND the hard stuff. Even the mistakes. You can learn from them and share your lessons with others. The stuff that goes your way and the stuff that doesn't. It's ALL helpful for you. You can use everything that happens in your life to help you get where you want to be. You know why?"

They nodded up and down and had big smiles on their cute, little faces:

"Because we're ninjas."

"That's right. You are. And you know what? Mom is, too. My mom and dad didn't have to be perfect people. They did great things and they did hurtful things. The hitting hurt me and I forgave them. And I learned, from how I was raised, that I didn't want to spank you so, we haven't done that, have we?" They both shook their heads emphatically.

Seth said, "And you don't scream or swear at us either."
Caleb said, "Well, you do raise your voice sometimes and I don't like that, but you don't scream and you don't swear."

Well, not that they heard, anyway. Their father would have a different answer.

"Fair enough, Bud." I tousled his hair and kissed his head, assuring him that I heard his heart. "Thanks for letting me know the whole truth. I'll work on that. I'm sorry."

He looked up at me with a confident nod and a forgiveness I could feel to my bones.

"Guys, I chose to learn from my parents doing great things and not so great things. Everything that happened made me smarter, more caring, and stronger. That's what ninjas do. They use everything -- not just the good things."

They were starting to get squirmy so, I knelt down and opened up my arms, where they ran for our big group ninja hug.

It's easy to forget the powerful ninja we are, when we're older. It's so easy to get stuck on the rock of who abused and hurt us, the limb of which relationship didn't work out, and who broke a promise to us.

It's easy to define ourselves by our mistakes and our failings instead of taking the lessons, focusing on our strengths, and moving on.

If I had stopped playing music on that day I had played the wrong song, the world would have missed not only my music, but my soul that goes with it. And I would have missed using those muscles of self-forgiveness, resilience, and lesson-learning that help me be who I am today.

My life didn't end that day because of playing Send in the Clowns

Or the day that I failed a test
Or the day that I went through abuse
Or the day that I lost it with my spouse
Or the day I got pulled over for a ticket...

My life carried on -- not without its bumps
And not because it was easy
But because it helped me be strong.

I learned how to jump off of those rocks
And climb on to those limbs
And jump to those higher places in myself
That see life as 'good'
(Even when it's hard)
And to see me as powerful
(Even when I don't feel like I am).

Not because it's all easy
But because I'm a ninja.

Just like Caleb and Seth.

And

Just like you.

11
Don't Waste the Pain

Speaking of ninjas, I was sitting across from one of my brilliant and beautiful friends in a coaching session. She had been the heroic single mom, raising amazing kids, after her ex had done not so amazing things -- capsizing their marriage and devastating the trust.

"What do you want out of this time -- and who do you want to be while you're walking through it?" I asked during our intention-setting time of our meeting.

Margo drew a deep breath and closed her eyes for a second in contemplation before she locked eyes with mine,

"I just don't want to waste the pain, Stacey. If it's going to be hard, I want it to be worth it and to learn the lessons that are in this pain now."

I loved the rock-star poetry and commitment I was hearing. It conjured such admiration for my friend who had already been through so much.

I don't know about you -- but when I'm tired and already feel like my emotional cup is full, I like to run away from the pain, avoid the pain, anesthetize the pain, and at the least, pretend it's not there.

I'd like to eat it away, drink it away, social media it away, phone call it away.

Which doesn't really work because pain oozes. If you don't take care of it when life is pressing on you, you can pretend all you want, but it's going to seep out the sides.

Somewhere
Everywhere
And it's going to be messy.

In that bitchy, cranky way to others -- to people like the waitress at the restaurant, or your kids or your partner.

It oozes out on the freeway, at the parent-teacher meeting and on the business call.

On the first dates with the new guy or the job interview.

Or in that depressing, "I don't want to get out of bed -- pretty much *ever*" kind of way.

Pain finds a way of making itself known. It has flares that it uses when we try to abandon it on the desert island of our distractions.

So, to have someone say to me, "I don't want to waste it" is a monumental, Olympic-gold-winner ninja kind of soul that's sitting in front of me.

My friend, Sam, is that kind of woman, too.

She went through a carjacking (where she was held at gunpoint), a divorce, and finding out her four year-old had cancer, all within a couple of years of each other.

This woman is able to sit with you in your pain, and embrace the depth of a situation like no one else can.

She doesn't avoid pain. She doesn't get to.

She has to take her daughter every six months for follow-up, and feel that mix of incredible gratitude that Ryan's still here at 10 years-old -- and that mix of punch-you-in-the-gut, abject dread, waiting for test results to return to make sure her daughter's still clear.

Sam is one of the bravest, most beautiful women I know.

She doesn't waste the pain.

She uses it.

She's stronger, smarter, more compassionate, and more of a fierce and loving advocate than she's ever been.

She doesn't live running away from life, she lives it head on -- and when she looks at you with the intensity of her green eyes, you know that this woman will fight to the death on what matters most.

She's let pain prioritize her life in the very best sense: People first -- every freaking thing else, second.

Her pain became her fuel instead of her enemy.

Women like Margo and Sam are heroes to me.

My friend, Carissa, had listened to me tell of the latest health report from my doctor and what the suggested regimen was to get me back on course. It was expensive and it was intense.

She was quietly taking it all in and then, broke the silence with one of her traditional cut-to-the-chase responses, "Well, you can have it take 5 months or 5 years to heal. Your choice."

So freaking aggravating.
So freaking true.
How many times have I drug out the hard thing for a long time,

because I didn't want to deal with the intensity of it for a short time?

Why do I so often forget, that when I surrender and breathe through what is going on, I'm able to move through it faster?

Another girlfriend of mine confessed something similar to God: "I want to stop avoiding the pain of what is true. Please help me to face the pain that I'm running away from."

She had inklings in her inner being that she was spending her energy holding back some hurtful truths. The emotional exhaustion mixed with Divine Grace, allowed her to pray that willing prayer.

Her life broke wide open after that. Lots of painful stuff came up. She faced it head-on with prayer and friendship and a vulnerability that allowed her to completely enjoy her life in a way that she never had before.

Pain-avoidance takes so much time away from our life,

And so much life away from our time.

We sat at the table, together as a family. It was quiet. My 12 year-old had pulled himself out of school because he'd reached his tolerance with the bullying issue. Too many grown-up agendas and administration issues meant that he had to make the mature, self-honoring choice to leave.

"I can't do it anymore, Mom…" I saw his strength in his weariness.

I want to be like him when I grow up.

In order to preserve the vast amount of deep good he had experienced for 5 years at his school, while processing the deep hurt that had gone on and worsened in the last year, I came up with an idea.

A blessing candle.

Good lord knows we have enough candles in our life so, I pulled one out and sat us all around it after dinner one night.

We had been having a lot of family meetings lately so, the boys settled in quickly, "I know this has not been our favorite time. And I know that we wish it were different. I also know that we, as powerful ninja people have the power to make the hard things into the good things."

My tribe was quietly sitting and listening while the dishwasher hummed in the kitchen behind us.

"So, one of the ways that I know how to help turn things around -- and to turn me around -- is to remember that I have a super power."

The boys looked up at me with wide-eyes.

12 year-olds and 10 year-olds still believe in superpowers.

My 47 year-old was pretty wide-eyed too.

"My superpower is blessing." I felt the room deflate a bit, "No wait... you'll see, it's pretty important. And Rock, you'll see that you have it, too."

Now, everyone was re-interested again.

"You know how when I make a mistake, or am cranky or mean? You tell me that you don't like it when I talk that way. But then, after, you come up to me and say, 'I love you, Stacey Robbins, and I bless you.' it makes me feel like I'm not just a failure but I'm also the good things, too."
I looked into my husband's eyes.

"You are so many good things -- even when you're being Ms. Cranky Pants." He winked at me.

"Yeah. But I forget that sometimes, until you remind me."

"When you bless me, Rock, I walk differently. I know you're not happy with me, but your blessing helps me to turn my attitude around. Thank you, honey."

Rock sat across the table in the dimly lit dark and smiled to me. The boys felt proud.

"But not only that," I continued, "when I bless someone who is being unkind, or I bless a hard situation -- I end up feeling really powerful, too! Like the hard thing isn't bigger than me, but my goodness is bigger than what was hard -- and I can even see it differently because I remember my power to use it. You know, like ninjas do."

The boys smiled.

"So, I thought about taking time to use our superpowers each day as we heal through this. That we would take a time to go around the table four times.

The first time we will Bless Those We Love -- you know, the easy people -- you, your brother, Daddy, me." I pointed to Caleb. "It's easy to bless the people we love, right?"

Everyone nodded in agreement.

"The second pass we will Bless Those in Need -- you know how we see Miss Alice going around with her walker? Her hips hurt a lot. Or remember when Ms. Rachel had migraines? Or remember the homeless man we saw on the street? We will take time to bless them." The kids got faraway looks in their eyes, thinking about who they could bless.

"And then, we're going to Bless Those Who Are Hard to Travel With -- you know, those difficult people in our life. The person who makes us angry or hurts us, who misunderstands us or we don't agree with -- or just makes us feel like we're not our best selves when we're with them. We all have people like that -- Daddy does, I do, and you boys do, too."

We all sat, bobbing our heads up and down. We all really understood.

"So, guys, here's the thing: In life, there are always going to be those people -- someone we don't agree with or like -- or who hurts us. But we will always have our power with us, too. The power to bless our situations and those people so that we can handle it."

Captain Justice (a.k.a Caleb) said, "Does that mean we're saying it's okay what they did?" He had tears at the brim of his eyes.

I reached out to touch his hand, "Absolutely not. It's not okay. We can feel hurt and cry and be mad and feel like it's unfair. Those are really normal, human feelings. And, just so you know, I'm not saying we should feel good about people being mean or hurtful. Not at all. That would be kinda crazy, right?"

We all agreed.

"I'm just saying that when we say, 'I bless this hard person or hard situation' that we are saying, 'I'm not going to let this make me less of who I am, I am going to use this to make me even more of the amazing person I am here to be. This won't make me weaker. This will make me stronger.' "

I squeezed his hand and he squeezed back. He understood.

"And you know what guys? I believe we have this really incredible invisible energy -- that when we bless others, we can actually help to shift the way things go. Things can change because we're using our power to bless."

Caleb said, "That's like Dr. Emoto -- the guy who put paper with loving words on the water jars and the water became more healing. But when he put hateful words on, the water changed and got bad."

I love when kids give better examples than we do.

I remembered, "Yes! Remember how the molecules changed and the jars with loving words had the most beautiful water molecules! And the ones that didn't, looked like demon faces and weird."

Rock said, "People are made up of like 70% water. What do you think would happen if we blessed them?"

Caleb said, "We could make a difference."

I looked at him, "That's our superpower, Cay. That's what we're going to do right now."

We went around the table, Blessing Those We Love, Blessing Those in Need, and with some tears, Blessing Those Who Were Hard to Travel With.

As we finished wiping our eyes for the painful parts mixed with the powerful parts, Seth looked up at me, "Momma, you said there were four? We just did three."

I smiled at him, "Fourth time is Blessings on Us. Blessings on my mind and my big heart, blessings on the cellulite on my thighs and my gift for words. Blessings on what I see and don't see, on what I know and don't know. Blessings on Me."

"It's important to remember that we have the power to bless ourselves."

Caleb said, "Like when I was four years-old and I sneezed. Everyone was busy and no one said, 'Bless You, Caleb!' And I was upset. You came to the table where I was sitting and you said, 'Caleb, you always have the power to bless you -- even if no one else remembers, too.' That's why I say 'I bless me!' every time I sneeze!"

"Caleb!" I squeezed his face in my hands and kissed his 12 year-old, salty face, "That's it, exactly!"

Seth said, "Well, I don't know if we should make ourselves last, maybe we should make ourselves first in the blessing."

I smiled at him, "There are no rules in this -- do it in whatever order you want -- the point of it is to just remember that no matter what happens outside of us, that we have this amazing super power within us."

I still don't love pain. Honestly, who does...

Wait, don't answer that. We all know some interesting, kinky people and you know that's not what I'm talking about.

I'm just saying that pain avoidance is life avoidance -- because life has some pain built right into the fabric of it:

Childbirth
Cutting Teeth
Growing Taller
Relationships
Death
(Did I mention Relationships?)
Pain is a big revealer: It shows us where we are strong and where

we still need to grow stronger. And then, when we use the pain, it can give us strength. It illuminates to us where we turn when things get hard, and when we run, and why. The strength that pain gives is unique to every other thing we experience in life. I needed it when my 3 year-old went grey for 36 hours before we found out about the hole in his heart -- and when my preteen was being ripped apart by some of his peers -- and now, this sacred and unwieldy time of the teenage years when the emotions can go from 0-60 in about 2 seconds flat. Pimples included - no extra charge.

I need to remind myself of my heroic girlfriends who have stood strong in the face of the hardship and remember Winston Churchill's wisdom that one of the greatest ways past, is through.

Avoiding the inevitable is just prolonging the suffering.

I'm going to remember these great women and take their stories and strength with me -- reminding me that when life runs into us (or we run into life) that we don't have to spend our energy wishing the inevitable lessons weren't there. We can just bravely say in the face of them,

"I don't want to waste this."

We can light a candle
And get still, to reflect
To use this time to strengthen who we are

And remember that we have this deep, abiding power
To open that space inside of our heart

And to bless.

12
Where Love Is

I met Joanne while she was working at a makeup counter in Nordstrom inside of the renowned South Coast Plaza. It's an upper crust, kinda hip, slightly snooty, shopping destination in Southern California.

Joanne looked more than a little out of her element in conservative Orange County with her long dark hair (instead of bleach blonde), harsh make up, biker-style black, sleeveless leather vest, and totally ripped arms with tats. It seemed like she drew the short straw at the trendy LA store and had to go behind the "Orange Curtain" for a day.

Standing there finishing the make-up on a client, she reminded me of Linda Hamilton in the second "Terminator" movie with all her kick-ass grit and rough edges showing.

Which is probably why I liked her immediately.

It was my turn to be in her chair. We did the brief introduction thing and as she was doing God-only-knows-what with the brushes and colors on my face, Joanne started telling me about her life:

Single mom.
Two boys (both young teens).
Ex is a jerk. (Her words, not mine).

The boys live with her but they're cranky about it. Over and over these kids pursue their dad and want to hang with him but he doesn't call, cancels often, and is pretty uninvolved in general. And here's Joanne, picking up the pieces of the broken hearts of her proud boys

-- who are learning to be disconnected men -- all because they've got this itch with their dad that nothing else can scratch.

I could feel Joanne's frustration. Under those deep lines filled with designer cover-up, there was a woman who loved her kids and was hurting for their hurt. She pulled away to study my face, then blew the air out of tight lips as if she had just dragged on a cigarette, and said, "Stacey, I know they want what they want with their dad, but he's just not giving it to them. I'm the one who's always there for them but they end up angry at me because he's not around to get angry at. They just don't get it. I've told them, 'Don't go where you think love should be, guys -- you're not gonna find it there -- you gotta go where love is.' "

I think I stopped breathing for a second when her words connected to my heart.

Don't go where you think love should be;

Go where love is.

I had no idea that underneath all the tats, leather, and heavy-handed makeup, there was a hidden Buddha made of gold.

I didn't always go where love was.

Especially with God.

Let me back up: I think our family represents God when we're young. We come straight out of the chute, after being with the Divine, and our family will either confirm the higher messages of who we are or they will contradict them.

And likely, in most families, both happen.

If you come out with this divine imprint of "You're amazing, here to love and be loved."

And you get the message from your family, "You're amazing if you agree with me and loyal to me. If you don't, you're not. And if you aren't loyal to me -- and aren't willing trade out your truth for my truth, then, I won't give you love."

That kind of stuff will mess you up.

And will likely send you straight into the arms of some weird version of God that tells you the same thing.

So, looking back, it made sense that I would go to churches where there was a mix of wonderful and crazy. Because that was the mix of what I grew up in.

I loved the great parts of family and church -- community, food, music, serving others -- but it's not the great parts that undo us.

It's those awful undertow messages we get in the great ocean of life, like:

There's something wrong with you if you don't agree, or comply
There's something wrong with you if you question or doubt
There's something wrong with you if you love people we said you shouldn't.

The ocean of love and good stuff draws you into it, but the undertow of conditional love, based on you being less of you, will drag you out into deep waters and threaten your life.

You, not being you, risks the life of your soul.

I went to church, loving Jesus.

He and I had a good relationship. He was cool, he dug me, he helped me, I was thankful.

But when someone tells you that loving Jesus means:

You pray this way
Vote this way
Sing this way
Talk this way
Give your money this way
(Don't show your cleavage this way)
Hang out with these people and not those people, this way

And all that other stuff,
Jesus gets lost in the rules.

I don't think Jesus asked us to do too much:

"Love God. Love each other."

"And if you do any of that good, juicy stuff for each other, you just did it for God."

Easy.

I mean not easy, sometimes, but definitely not this long list of Thou Shalls and Thou Shall Nots that we make for each other.

I get it: When I feel free in my love, I just want people to be free and uniquely them. I feel very Jesus-y and non-judgy.

But when I get afraid, I start making rules.

Lots of them.

Just ask my husband.

When I feel hurt and my trust is broken -- I get very rules-y. My guard goes up and I start saying things like, "If you love me, you'll do this, thus, and so..."

It makes it very hard for the person (okay, my husband) to show me love when I've set up an Olympic-style obstacle course of hurdles for him to jump over.

And then, you know what happens? He's not living his life, he's living for my insecurities.

And I'm not living my life, I'm watching to see if he's running the race right or not.

And that's no life for either of us.

My friend, Dr. John Townsend, who co-wrote the ground-breaking book Boundaries said it best in a marriage talk he gave one day: "To the extent that you control, is the extent that you limit love in your life."

The brilliance of his words make me choke on every idea of love I've tried to swallow.

I thought I had to change and be less for some people, or change and be more for others -- all the while not really being me,

For me.

John's words ring true, because, here's the deal: Love is a free thing so, if you're trying to do something crazy for someone who's willing to trade *your* very essence for *their* acceptance -- that's not love -- that's control, and that's not free. It's not love if you have to stop being you. It's not free if it's given as a reward for good behavior.

A gold star on the forehead when you're in kindergarten is a reward for good behavior.

Less time in jail is a reward for good behavior.

But love?

Love is a great inspiration
But it's a terrible reward.

And any person, place, or god that makes you bark like a seal in order to get anything, is likely giving you more fish than love.

The conflicting messages are harder than the outright lies.

In church, I was told that I was made in the image and likeness of God. Awesome. But, at the same time, I was sent this message that I was a worm and worth nothing.

I was so confused.

So, is God a worm like me?
Or am I amazing like him?
And if Jesus died for me
But I'm worth nothing

Why would God be mean enough to make Jesus die for nothing?

It didn't make sense.

I would have asked questions but I learned from watching others that you got burned for asking questions. Not in hell. But from the leadership who believed that questions equalled insubordination. They would rain the hell of rejection on you, especially if you were considered a leader in the church, like I was.

Because it meant that you lacked faith - and your lack of faith displeased God.

Doubt and questions were seen as the disease of faith that you brought on yourself through your own sinful living or sinful thoughts. And because of all of that, the devil had entrance into your life and was obviously messing with your head about God.

Your doubt was a sin and something you needed to confess So that you could be healed.

And, if you didn't do it fast enough or thoroughly enough, you might risk your finances, your health, your children's safety or purity (and about 100,000 other things, including plagues and locusts) if you didn't hurry back to your right place of faith.

'Cause God might "get you."

I was taught to believe in a
Scary-ass god.

If he were a parent, people would be calling CPS to get the kids away from the crazy, abusive parent.

But in the churches I went to, we all showed up in droves to spend more time learning about a god who

You can never ask your questions.
Never have any doubts.

Unless they were those charming kinds of questions and doubts -- the one someone could still smile and see your purity and innocence in. I call them "Pottery Barn Messes".

Like the cover of the home design catalog that has a random rubber ball, and books strewn about in the living room.

Those neat kinds of messes.

But what about those really messy questions?

The stinky, skanky, of ill-repute, kinds of earthy and dirty questions where the doubt doesn't go away really fast, and in fact, the more questions you ask at first, the more complicated it all seems and the more you doubt and are tempted to walk away.

Like, "I know you (church) say we're supposed to change people who are gay and help them to know Jesus so that they can stop being gay -- but what if they're a better person than I am and live their lives with more kindness and Jesus-ness. And what if one of my sons ended up gay? Why would I take so much of my time, energy and our relationship to change him when I could just spend all my time loving him?"

Yeah.

If you have those, you better confess that as a sin, cast out the devil and get over that shit, like real quick, so that you don't have lightning bolts thrown on you or those you love.

I lived that way.
With that kind of god.

My prayers were as schizophrenic as I was:

"God, I know you're so awesome and I know you made the whole world, but I don't really trust you, because you freak me out with how you could punish me. But I'm really sorry I just said that, except that, if being totally honest, which I'm not, (which you already know, because you're God) I don't feel like I feel sorry or feel love or feel anything but afraid anymore -- so, I'm really more afraid, which is probably a lack of faith so, please forgive me of my sins of having no

faith and…"
Oh my god.

Seriously?

I was messed up for a long time.

Thinking that I should find love in the crazy theologies and the crazy relationships

But I couldn't.

Because I couldn't find love in me.

———————————

Trying to find your way back home to you, when you're middle aged, can be messy, unattractive -- and super-duper risky.

Especially when heaven is hanging in the balance.

That's scary for people who've lived like heaven was the goal and hell was the really, really bad, only other alternative.

So, as if facing the realities of cellulite, moodiness, and anxiety weren't hard enough to deal with in the here and now, I had to worry about the whole "forever and ever, amen" part, too.

It made me edgy. I didn't know how to talk to the god I was dealing with so, I considered this idea:

What if he's not real? What if that god isn't even a real god -- the one I've been dealing with -- so, I leaned in with some curiosity:

What if I just divorced that crazy, punishing, confusing idea of god and

started over?

I decided to talk to the ceiling to see if a new god might reveal himself, herself -- itself.

I drew a deep breath of forgiveness for everyone involved (including yours truly) in bringing me the ideas that had led me to the verge of this existential nervous breakdown, and I just started talking to this possibly good, non-scary God,

"Okay. I don't know exactly who you are but I'm pretty sure you're not the asshole God I've made you out to be. This 'Part Policeman, Zeus, and Santa Claus' god that I had constructed between all I've gone through and all I've learned in church isn't really lining up with a god I want to do business with. So, would you please let me know who you really are?"

I spent two long and strong years in a state of restless stillness and questions. At times, especially in the beginning, it was completely unnerving. Where I felt like I was racing against a lit fuse on a stick of dynamite with the theme music to "Mission Impossible" in the background -- trying to find answers about GodHeavenJesusDeathHell before it was too late, "or else…" That part was hard. The part where I wanted to have an answer, yesterday -- about forever.

My adrenal glands were exhausted.

Other times, I could relax and surrender more -- and felt a little more playful and less of a nerve-ending. Those times, it was sort of like making mudpies when I was a kid -- the process was a monumental mess, nothing is edible when you're done, and you likely need to throw every stitch of clothing and your shoes away (and bonus, you will have mud in cracks and crevices that you didn't even know you had).

But all the while you're in the wet earth, you didn't realize that you were grounding yourself in nature, nourishing your body with minerals that are in it, that your brain registered all this play as joyful meditation -- and that you were actually happy doing something that resulted in nothing, but was part of your everything -- and there was great value in *that*.

God and I were making mudpies together in our conversations. It was a monumental mess of questions, doubts, anxiety and frustration, confessions, revelations, insomnia, and silence. Most of my beliefs got thrown out and I wound up, after quite an unraveling -- blissfully naked with the peace and lightness of God stuck in the places of my heart and mind that I didn't even know I had, when I felt him say these words to me one night, "I am Love. And you are Love, too."

I walked away with a "less is more" theology -- less hang-ups, less rules, less pressure; more of me and others to embrace, with a "God is Love. Love made You. You are Love, too" way of thinking.

I needed that desperately.

Because once I settled in to the fact that God was at home with me being exactly who I am,
I stopped chasing after people, places and things where I thought love should be.

Go where love is.

If Blake Shelton were a pastor, I'd go to his church.

It's not just because he's hilarious and sexy

(which he is)

*(which is SUPER uncomfortable for me to say because I only use the "sexy" word to describe my husband but I figured **you** think Blake is sexy so, I just slipped that in...*

You know...

*For **you**.)*

Or because he would likely be walking around with a grown-up sippy cup filled with whiskey while he preached his morning sermon, strolling around the stage in his cowboy boots,

(which he likely would)

And it's not because he has this amazing track record in marriage or has a spotless personal reputation in the music biz

(which he doesn't)

Nope.

There's just something about him...

Something that just makes you feel like his love is this close (I'm sitting here with my palms facing each other so near together that you can't even see a slit of light between them) and it's *that* love, that is going to somehow right every wrong that has ever been done to you.

As playful and fun and downright goofy as he can be, you just feel like if the building is on fire, and you're loved by Blake, he's gonna pick your ass up first, and get you the hell out of there.

I can feel it through the TV screen.

And I don't think it's just me. I think that the dads who have their teenage daughters audition for The Voice feel it, too. And the women who have been hurt in a relationship or have lost someone they've loved and aren't quite yet healed.

There's something about his "Gosh, golly gee" Gomer Pyle innocence that meets his modern John Wayne "No one ain't gonna hurt you on my watch" kind of vibe that makes you feel like his love is gonna keep you safe.

It's not going to promise you that everything is gonna be perfect.

It just makes you feel like he'll be there if it's not.

It's the kind of love you want to run to.

It's a God kind of love
It's a people kind of love
It's a messy kind of love
It's a healing kind of love.

That's why, I told my boys: "Don't look for someone who says they believe in God as the sign of trustworthy love -- look at someone's life and notice if you see love."

Someone who knows how to forgive themselves and forgive others and move on without holding a grudge against either one.

Someone who can laugh at themselves when they trip over lint and not blame the devil for sticking its invisible shoe out.

Someone who can have a drink when they're with you without feeling like they need to apologize for being more human and less spiritual.

Being human is spiritual.

God didn't make us into ghosts, he made us into humans.

Our humanity is pretty divine -- and I want to be around people who see and live that.

It took me a long time, and I'm still on that journey -- to get rid of the love/hate relationship I have with me that I was raised in and churched in.

I'm returning to that straight-out-of-the-chute kind of love -- and the more I do, the less I run to crazy places or make people jump crazy hurdles for me.

But that's been quite a trip I've taken.

If Joanne's boys were in front of me, I'd want to say this: "Sweethearts, know this: that your dad may love you, but there might be too much undertow in his ocean right now. And that doesn't make him wrong or bad -- and it doesn't make him less of an ocean -- it's just not the right time to step into those waters.

And while you're sorting that out, know this: You didn't do anything to make him be this way and his lack of giving to you doesn't mean that you did anything to deserve it. That's his shit to work out. Don't wait for him, but stay open to him -- and just keep your eyes on the whole truth:

You are from God
And God is Love
So you are too.

Once you settle into the Love that you are,
You'll have a much easier time going where Love is."

13
The Yahtzee Principle

I left them in England with a note attached:

"If you have size 10 feet and toes of steel, be my guest."

I bought the pair of shoes in haste before the trip.

"Why in haste?" you ask? Because on Tuesday, I thought my plane was leaving from New York on Thursday and found out it was leaving on Wednesday. Life got a little hairy for 24 hours and I made the mistake of picking the cute size 10's with a slight wedge instead of the practical and ugly size 11 flats.

So, I abandoned them in England before our flight down to Italy and left myself with one pair of 7 year-old, butt-ugly sneakers.

What I really wanted was a cute pair of Italian sandals to walk the cobblestone streets of Florence.

I actually didn't want them. I needed them. The sneakers were great, unless you were walking 7 miles a day (which I was). After about 4 miles, they got hot, sweaty and made your feet pulse -- as if they were hanging out at a disco with a loud bass thumping underneath them. Plus, they weren't cute. I couldn't wear half of my outfits with them without looking like a frumpy, dumpy American tourist.

I wanted to look "international."

Sigh.

And so, the hunt began...

For the perfect, Italian-made *sandolo* for a great price, since I had already spent my shoe budget on the pair I had orphaned 1,000 miles ago.

I asked a few people where to buy a 'reasonably-priced, adorable pair of shoes' but I kept getting lost. I wondered if I was missing all the great stores because I had landed with jet lag, my period, two grumpy children, and throbbing feet.

I walked.

And I walked.

And then, for good measure, I walked some more.

I either found ugly flats that felt great (I did not come to Italy to buy ugly shoes. I could have done that in America, before I left) or gorgeous chunky, stylish heels from Brazil (did you know that so many Italians buy shoes made in Brazil?) for 300 euros.

I was not happy.

From the way my tired brain was seeing things, there were only about 6 shoe stores in all of Florence. I could find leather handbags or fabulous scarves -- which I didn't want or need -- at every turn. If I had a euro for every stand that sold 'lampredotto' (a Florentine specialty sandwich made up of the lining of the cow's 4th part of the stomach -- ick) that I had no interest in eating, I would be a rich woman. If I were in the market for a piece of ceramic-something painted with the Fleur de lis pattern, I could have bought a storehouse full.

But shoes?

It was like they all ran away and were hiding from me.

Most of my friends on social media couldn't believe my problem with finding something cute and comfortable to put on my feet *while I was in Italy*. One of my friends who knew the area recommended an outlet where I finally landed a darling pair of black, leather sandals.

"They are notta greata leather," said the ridiculously handsome tall, dark, and very Italian salesman who shrugged his shoulders in a 'meh' sort of way, "But theya are-a okay. I sell them alla day long, and theya are Italian."

I appreciated his honesty and the 39 euro price tag and put them on my feet. They were too stinkin' cute and about 10 steps later, they started to break me in. My virgin skin was about to have Made In Italy blisters.

But I didn't care. I had shoes. I could see my cute toe rings.

I was *happy*.

Wouldn't you know that the minute I left the store with the darling black sandals on my feet, all the shoe stores started jumping out and waving to me.

———————

You would have thought I'd have learned my lesson – but maybe it was the UTI and head cold that I got on the heels of the jet lag, period, and grumpy kids -- all in the same week -- (are we having fun yet?) but after almost 10 days of being on our trip, I entered the "I need a lipstick" version of The Hunger Games.

Wearing my new leather *sandolos* and sporting the appropriate amount of blister bandages on both feet, I now needed to take care of my lips.

This would probably be a good time to explain that we all only took one small carry-on for our trip. The guys wore a single back-pack and I had a small stroll-y thing. We each brought barely a blip of anything and we figured we'd buy what we needed when we got there.

So, I brought my so-empty-I-have-to-dig-it-out-with-a-Q-tip remnant of my all-time favorite lipstick, all the way to Italy. Lipstick Queen's "Nude Sinner" was the name my girlfriends absolutely adored and my mother hated. It's the perfect shade of rosey-red brown that is delicious and makes my skin look all glowy and warm. I get stopped at least once a day and asked what color I'm wearing -- and then, I get the complete joy of answering,

"Nude Sinner. It's my favorite! Don't you love it?"

And I can feel my New Jersey, Italian mother dying a thousand deaths from thousands of miles away.

There I was in Florence, on the hunt for my perfect lipstick.

Lo-and-behold, 10 more stores and 3 more blisters later, they don't carry my brand in Firenze.

Nude statues. Yes.

Nude Sinners. No.

My mother said via-text, "Good Lord, get an Italian-made lipstick there. I'm sure they'll have something that's absolutely stunning. Italians make the best of everything."

(Did I mention we're 100% Italian, that my mother's slightly biased -- and that she was probably doing a rosary for me to own a lipstick with a new name?)

Again, like the shoes, I could find nothing.

I found a MAC store, which I normally love for their deeply-pigmented colors but ended up with one that wasn't really "me."

I was not happy,

but the deed was done.

I sighed in resignation.

Again, as if by some strange magic, the moment I had my new lips on, every Italian-made lipstick with the most GORGEOUS colors seemed to be in every window.

I rolled my eyes, tucked the MAC lipstick a little lower in my purse, and bought one made in Milan (now breaking my lipstick budget) and headed back to our rental.

It had been so rainy that day in Firenze that we were starting to become mildewed. My boys had watched me act like a crazy person -- the first few days looking for shoes and now, a week later, hunting for lipstick -- and watching me be Miss Grumpy Pants in the process of both. We were all more than fussy when we returned to our apartment at the end of that long, wet day.

———————

After showers and food that night, the boys told us that they wanted friends.

Who speak English.

Who are their age.

(And who don't spend their days dragging them around Italy, shoe and lipstick shopping - was the unspoken message for me.)

It was the plight we were experiencing as we were on our Magical, Healing Adventure and new to the life of World Schooling (where you use travel as a means to learn). The boys are such social creatures and they had been through a lot of changes in that last year: Caleb had dealt with the bullying thing at his old school and Seth dealt with the remnants of some negative influences at the new school -- which led to bad attitudes, on his part, which led to wanting to pull every freakin' curl out of his head, on my part. It was exhausting. We all needed healing from where it hurt, but as author and Franciscan priest, Richard Rohr explains, "The process of going from order to re-order has to pass through disorder." We were in the icky part of 'disorder.'

The boys were on each other's nerves
We (the parents) were boring
And the kids missed their friends.

Oh lord...

It broke my heart in about a million places to think that, while we were in this amazing place called Italy -- with all its incredible art, music, history, and food -- that I was fretting because I couldn't find any shoes or lipstick -- and they were fretting because they hadn't found any friends.

I went to bed, meditating about it all and then, slept on it for the night. I find those practices, like meditation, comforting to me when my heart hurts for my boys. It's a deep place where that ache lives, and verbal processing just doesn't seem to cut it -- so I get quiet, go within, and pray.

The next morning, I woke up with so many thoughts, quotes, and stories for Thing 1 and Thing 2 that I couldn't wait to share. So, that night, after dinner I sat them down:

"Remember how when we got here, I was a crazy lady trying to find a pair of shoes?"

They rolled their eyes at the question. Caleb said, "Yeah. And you found that pair that gave you blisters for a week. You used up all the really good blister Band Aids, by the way."

I nodded and pointed my index finger at him and then, his brother, "That's right. So nobody's allowed to get any more blisters, okay?"

They smiled as I went on,

"And remember how after that, I was a crazy lady trying to find the perfect lipstick?"

Seth said, "Yeah. And then, you found one you didn't like and bought that and then, found all these other ones you really liked."

Caleb shook his head at the reminder of how I dragged them through Florence and how he lived to tell the tale.

I went on to share, "Guys, it seemed that the harder I wanted something, the more I couldn't find it, because I was looking at it from the place of 'It's a problem that I don't have this...'

It's a problem that I can't find shoes.
It's a problem that I can't find the lipstick.

That's the way my mind was processing it. I wasn't just looking for those things because they would be good things to have, I was looking for those things because I didn't feel good without them."

We all sighed.

I reminded them of one of my favorite games: Yahtzee -- where you roll the five dice and try to get certain number combinations in order to get your points. A Yahtzee is when you roll all five dice with the same number on each die. It's the highest set of points you can get -- because it's the hardest odds to get them all to match up.

"You know how when you're trying to get a Yahtzee because you're behind in points and you're looking for a Yahtzee to make up the difference?" They both nodded, knowingly. "You get really tight and stressed and roll *anything* but a Yahtzee."

They stared at me. Caleb motioned his hand impatiently for me to keep going.

"But then, there are other times where you're feeling ahead of the game -- or you don't really care if you win or lose -- you're just relaxed and having fun -- and then, you end up with like FIVE Yahtzee's in that game -- more than what you even needed!"

They both nodded, enthusiastically. We had all had those moments and would get giddy at how unbelievable it was to roll so many Yahtzees without even trying so hard.

They got it. I could tell.

"So, guys," I looked at each one, "you say you want friends…"

Caleb pursed his lips in understanding, "I've been treating it like it's a problem that I can't find friends but maybe if I just wanted it, without needing it to make me happy, then, I would find some kids to hang out with…" his voice trailed off in reflection.

Seth said, "Yeah. It's almost like being too needy about something puts a lot of pressure on everything and blocks you from getting it."

"Like me," I pointed to myself, "When I relaxed about it, I found a lot of shoes and a lot of lipstick."

Caleb reminded me, "That was ridiculous, by the way, Mom, and I am NOT doing that again."

I nodded, "I know. It was and I'm sorry."

I felt badly -- I hate learning lessons on their watch.

"Oh guys, wait, please hear this: There's nothing wrong with wanting friends or lipstick or shoes or to roll a Yahtzee. It's not about that. Those are all fine things. I'm just noticing that when I already feel good about me and my life -- those other good things appear. But when I think that somehow, something that I'm looking for will make me more valuable, then those things seem to be harder to find."

We had a moment of quiet while the truth of that sank in for all of us.

Some people call it "The Law of Attraction" -- when we draw good things toward us from a whole and happy place so, maybe we could call the opposite, "The Law of Attachment" -- when we're repelling the very things we want because we're attached to some idea about having them.

The minute something means too much, for the wrong reason, it seems that we get attached.

If I HAVE to get married in order to feel like I matter vs. I want to get married because it can be a great way to share life with another person -- doesn't that carry a different energy?

If I HAVE to have children in order to feel like a complete woman vs. I want to have children because it feels like something I'm excited to do -- isn't that a different thing?

It's the story of my life: the things that I didn't put pressure on myself to have, "or else" -- just showed up with ease. Like having a husband or a music career or friendships or this trip to Europe -- those things seemed to have found their way to me. Not without effort, but without attachment and judgment.

I didn't have this idea that doing this thing (like professional music) or having this thing (like a husband) would make me "more," "better," or "good."

I didn't judge that I was unworthy to have it
And I didn't judge that it was impossible to have.

I just wanted it -- or at the very least was open to it -- and I worked to make it happen.

So much of my life has flowed that way.

But then, there have been the places where I judged myself as lacking and that the thing (whatever that thing was - losing weight, a certain amount of money, a car with leather seats) would make me feel more whole.

The more I wanted something to fill me or complete me, the more elusive it became.

It reminds me of those hot, humid summers growing up in Connecticut. I would be playing in our pool and would spy a toy on the other end, in the water. I'd paddle my arms in an effort to woo it toward me. The harder my hands paddled, the further away this thing would get. Even though I could have easily swum to it, I only wanted that toy to come in that way. Frustrated, I'd finally give up, climb onto the floating lounge, and forget about the toy -- and promptly bump into it about a million times.

There's something about letting go of the "I have to have this or else -- and in this way or else" that seems to give space for that thing you want to move toward you.

The metaphysical world calls that "attachment" when we act like we need a certain something in order to be whole -- it comes from judgment ("I will be better or worse without this") and judgment comes from fear ("If I don't have this, I won't be loved").

Judgment seems to be a repellent and wonky motives seem to make it harder to have what I want -- and harder to enjoy, once I muscle it into my life.

Because it's all coming from fear. And fear is such a black hole kind of energy.

But there's another way: Commitment. Being committed to what is possible is another way of saying, "I want this. I'm not defined by having it or not. I feel good about it. I'm committed to having it. I'm not better or worse for having it, I just believe that anything is possible and in that state of anything is possible, I choose this."

That's the game to play and win.

Whether it's with wanting a spouse
Or wanting to have kids
Whether it's wanting to buy a home
Or wanting a brand new car.

Whether it's about losing weight in your thighs
Or finding your favorite lipstick in Italy

The Yahtzee principle is the same:

When you feel like you're already enough
You'll have more than you ever need.

14
The Missing Peace

I couldn't find the damned thing.

This happens all the time with me. My husband hands me something like our new insurance card or car registration and, because he knows me says, "Put it in your wallet -- *now*."

I look at him, nod and smile -- and then, I promptly set it aside, and even pat it to assure it that I will be back for it later, *I promise* -- and voila! The hormones that affect my memory go into collusion with the same Force that steals socks from your dryer -- and suddenly, *it's gone.* I turn into the unintentional magician who makes important things disappear. It seems like half of my life ends up in the witness protection program -- this time it was my credit card.

Not just any credit card - *the* credit card. The one with the high limit that we hadn't used in forever but was there if we needed it. And we needed it...to pay a bill within 30 days and I couldn't find it.
Oh joy.

The internal conversations began:

Do I tell my husband and face the well-deserved, mini-lecture.

Or do I wait -- and just search high and low to find it myself and risk that, in the meantime, some ne'er-do-well is running up my card on pricey electronics and a first class ticket to my dream vacation?

Choices, choices...

I closed my eyes and in an "In with the good air, out with the 'Why

169

do I do this to myself?" meditation, my pride and I chose the latter. I tend to do that -- hide myself out until I can fix my mistakes. Then, I come back with the whole story. A sort of post-confessional with a great punchline of all the dramatic suspense and then, how it all worked out --

Ta-dah!

In the meantime, though -- pre-*ta-dah!* -- I get so afraid of letting anyone know the mistakes that I've made or the the thing that I've lost, that I go into Lone Ranger mode. It's stressful and stupid and I forget to remind myself:

Even the Lone Ranger had Tonto.

I could handle my little "Hide and Fix" program a lot better before I had children. You can be Lone Ranger when you don't have two small children making messes, stealing your brain cells, and talking incessantly, like the static you get when you're between two radio stations.

But now, in my mombie-zombie, post-apocalyptic, post-childbirth life, I just can't seem to keep it all together

Or to remember where I put things.

My life at 40, with two small children is mostly spent looking for what I've lost.

If anyone was silly enough to do a reality show on me, they would spend the majority of their time following me around and covering the most unflattering shots of my rearend, as I bend over (yet again) trying to find one of the many items that I've hidden from myself.

Yesterday, it was the DVD cover to a Charlie Brown video from the library.

I owe a king's ransom to the library for all of the "free" items I can't find when they're due. I held the kids hostage: *"We cannot go to the pool until we find this video cover!"* Thing 1 and Thing 2 dutifully fell in step behind me as we hunted high and low, in and out, and all around -- cleaning parts of the garage and all of the back of my car while we searched for this thing. After an hour and a half of deep knee bends and even deeper frustration, guess where we found it? Under *my* piled-over clothes, beside *my* bed, on *my* floor.

I deserve a spanking.

Seriously.

The credit card was a bigger deal for all the obvious identity theft reasons and it was starting to freak me out: One week, two weeks, and almost three weeks went by and there was still no credit card. I checked and rechecked my crazy over-stuffed wallet that also houses business cards, frequent buyer fro-yo punch cards, along with a host of receipts, gum wrappers (chewed gum, included) and random phone numbers with no names.

As if I had possibly missed it the first 34 times I had rifled through my deck, I chose to live out the definition of insanity, and went back to my wallet one more time, talking to myself the whole time in a slightly schizophrenic way:

"I know it's in here!" one part of me said, optimistically.

While the Nervous Nellie part of me was losing it, "Someone is flying MY dream trip to Italy and eating gelato on MY emergency credit card!"

It has to be in here! I demanded and pleaded to myself.

This time I did something different than the last 34 times. Instead of sifting through the pile in the direction it was facing me, I took each card and turned it over, looking at it front and back.

About halfway through, I flipped a card that was facing backwards and upside down and there it was. Plain as day. As my mother would have said, "If it were a snake, it would have bit ya."

Yes...

Bite me, indeed.

I'm not the only one who always feels like she's looking for something.

A few days later, my girlfriend, Michelle, asked the question burning inside of her, "Stace, so when am I going to start feeling peace? Is it ever going to come, or is life going to be this hard forever?"

I hated that she was asking me this question because she's amazing and working really hard without the reward of enjoying her life. Her life is both too much and not enough, filled with pretty-packaged disappointed expectations.

She wanted to have this kind of husband, but got that one. She wanted to have this kind of house, but got that one, she wanted to have these kinds of respectful children but got this brand of ungrateful ones. She wanted this kind of money and security but got that kind instead.

She's living with all the beautiful trappings of a modern life, but she's not happy.

It's like a fairytale gone wrong.

And each day, she rallies herself, thinking that this will be the day that the husband is on board, that the kids will approach her with kindness, and that she will feel like all is well with the world.

But another day goes by when it doesn't,
And it's not.

She plays the game that so many of us have found ourselves in --
some version of Hunger Games by our own choice -- where we're
playing to the death on some culturally manufactured game of
external happiness.

*If only we had THAT house and THAT amount of money in the bank
and THAT kind of relationship -- you know, that, over there -- then
we'd have peace.*

It's such a head game, this message of "not good enough" in our
society, that we forget that it's not the only message to live by.

Remember advertising classes in college? It's so much about the
psychology of "creating a need" -- whether it was for a new toothpaste,
a more concentrated laundry detergent, an improved spray cleaner-
something or other. And one day you wake up and look at your
"something" and think you need a different "other."

You start resenting the toothpaste you have because it's not the
whiter, brighter variety that you saw in the magazine. Instead of
being grateful for teeth to chew the food that you're grateful to have,
you spit out your old toothpaste in the sink like it failed you.

I've gone through this ad nauseum with my weight. I lived in my 20's
and some of my 30's like happiness was a number on the scale and
the size on the tag of my jeans. It took many years, but ultimately, I
did some significant processing that allowed me to take the bulk of
the pressure off of my hips and start living with freedom.

I tucked away the scale into the high part of the closet, since I realized
that I didn't need that number to tell me if I should be happy or not
-- and because I didn't want to measure me by a number when what
I really needed to get clear on was my inherent worth.

All of this outside struggle -- whether it's money, weight, fame, attention, or whatever -- it's just the distracted pursuit of a life that has no peace on the inside.

Because when you have peace, toothpaste is just toothpaste, a house is just a house, weight is just a number -- and none of it is the end of the world,

Because you weren't expecting any of it to be your whole world...

To be your happiness

To be your peace.

––––––––––––––––

My 4 year-old turned to his 6 year-old brother one day and called him a "Thing." This was before they thought it was cute that I called them "Thing 1" and "Thing 2"

Which of course sent my accuracy-driven 6 year-old into a "It's not so!" tizzy and the ensuing, "Yes, you are!" "No, I'm not!" went back and forth in a way that makes you want to drive your car off the edge of a cliff.

I looked into the mirror to catch his eye,

"Caleb, are you a 'thing'?"

"No." He sulked and looked out the window with his brows all squinchy.

"So, it's not true. You know you're not a 'thing' so, don't let your brother bust your chops."

He was silent.

"What are you made out of?" I asked my frowning first born, "Peanut fritters?"

"No." He rolled his eyes, still looking out the window.

"Bananas?"

"No." He shifted in his seat and exhaled like I was torturing him.

"Monkey butter??"

"Nooooo …" Little smile popped up and I watched him peek at me.

"Who made you, Caleb?"

"God." He said with an exasperated sigh.

Because they've heard this before, I could tell their minds were going into that "blah, blah, blah" mode so, I switched gears.

"Look guys…" I held up my hand and made a fist. "If I had sticks in my hand and I built a house, what would the house be made of?"

"Sticks." They answered together.

"If I had bricks in my hand, what would the house be made of?"

"Bricks."

"And if I had GOLD in my hand, what would the house be made of?"

"GOLD!" They were excited.

I brought my voice down to a whisper,

"Okay. So, if I were making a person and I had 'good' in my hands, what would the person be?"
They whispered together, "Good."

I got a little louder, "What if I had 'bad' in my hands?"

They got a little louder, too, "Bad!"

I got really big with my voice, "And what if I had Love in my hands?"

"Love!" They shouted and giggled.

"Guys, who made you again?"

They said, "God."

"What is God made of?"

"Love."

"So, if God is Love and Love made you from itself, what are you made of?"

"LOVE!"

You could practically hear the roar of the angels cheering in the Universe.

It was a sweet moment.

"So, when someone calls you a 'thing' are you really that or do they just not understand." I looked at Caleb in the mirror.

"They just don't understand."

"So, you don't need to let it bother you when someone calls you a name or gives you a hard time, do you?"

He shook his head, agreeing with me. "They just don't understand."

I peeked at the little squirt in the rearview and he looked back at me, "And by the way, Seth, that wasn't very kind to call your brother a 'Thing.'"

Seth nodded, his ringlets bobbing in a cartoonish way, but I just couldn't laugh or I'd risk blowing all the conviction he needed to feel.

"Thorry, Caleb." came the repentant lisp from my curly-haired wonder.

And all was well with the world, because in that moment, we were all reminded what was at our core.

Caleb let his brother get under his skin, because he forgot to occupy that space with the truth.

People can't get under our skin with their lies, when we are already filled with the truth.

And because we can't spend all our energy running around trying to make people stop the lie they're telling, we need to spend our energy on the truth we're believing.

Because those little lies grow up and get bigger when we do -- and because we believed the lies from the outside and took them in, we start looking for our happiness and peace outside of us, too.

Like Michelle, who was experiencing the frustration of placing her peace on external conditions. It wasn't working.

Because if we don't remember who we are
And where we're from
And what we're here to do

From the inside, out

We are going to spend our life wishing and waiting,
Instead of living and loving.

I know. I've tried doing it the other way.
That non-peaceful, doesn't-work, kind of way.

My journey reminds me of the story of the monks in search of the legendary Golden Buddha. The monks hunted high and low for the buddha that had the immense value. They'd leave their village and their buddha to search for the one they deemed "special."

One day, a monk was transporting their simple clay buddha and saw a crack in the clay. As he peered closer, he saw the shimmer of gold. As he continued to chip away, he discovered the golden buddha -- which had been in his village -- and in his midst the entire time.

The dissatisfaction in the search outside of ourselves can eventually turn to realizing the gold in our midst.

I've searched for peace in the same way that I've searched for my credit card -- expecting it to be where I thought it should be and to look a certain way: in the weight loss, financial gain, a clean house, and kids who actually sat down when we ate in a restaurant. But I kept missing it because that's not what peace looks like.

How do I know?

My ass got fat, my bank account got skinny, and my life got messy.

At some point I realized that if I kept waiting for conditions to be perfect in order to have peace, I was never going to have it. And because peace and happiness seemed to be best friends, I needed to shift where I was looking for them to be in order to have them both.

Once I realized true bliss wasn't waiting in the leather seats of a new car, I tried a different tack -- a spiritual one: I tried to find it chasing spiritual gurus and thought-leaders around the globe.

Guess what?

It's not there, either.

We can change what we're chasing after, but there's something in the chase that reflected one basic thing:

I didn't trust me -- to know who I was and what was best for me.

Because of that -- I didn't know how to be alone with me -- and in that, I strived to find some sense of trust and rest outside of me.

In something else - or someone else.

But it didn't work. *Because it's not supposed to.*

External things have limits.
Just like they're supposed to.

I had to stop running and stop striving.

That journey of being still, brought me a sense of inner trust, and because trust equals rest, and rest equals peace -- it was all part of me being okay with me.

No matter what size my jeans were
Or how well you thought about me

Or how many successes I achieved or mistakes I made.

This peace thing is an inside job.

It's not out there, it's in *here*.

It's in you.

And it's in me.

15
Non-GMO Spirituality

"Mom! Did you know that you're fat??"

In one unthinking moment, I made the mistake of showing the kids an episode of "The Biggest Loser" on the computer.

They kept looking at the screen, and then, back at me. In all of their wide-eyed innocence they tapped my arm, curious for an answer, "Mom, did you...?"

It just hadn't registered with them that I was something and they were not. That's one of the better parts of not raising your kids with television. We had taken it out of the house about 5 years before they were born when Rock and I were going through a hard time. A lot of the arguments were centered around the devastating effects of Mass Distraction in my husband's life and a desire to be more focused on what mattered most.

Trust me, I missed the Food Network and Martha Stewart -- and after having kids, there were days where I wished I could have just sat them down in front of Dora the Explorer while I cleaned or napped or drank wine, but the choice we made -- while not being irreversible -- was just one that we were committed to, whether it was inconvenient or not.

And because they didn't have the onslaught of media and all the accompanying indoctrinations, they didn't know that I was heavy and they were thin. They just knew I was mom and I loved them and that was that.

Which was kind of a nice reality to live in, let me tell you.

It was only a few years before when I heard them whispering behind me on the steps going up to the bedrooms to put away our clean clothes. We got to the top and I turned around with a "Yes? What's going on?" smile on my face.

Caleb, who was around 7 at the time turned to his little brother and then back at me,

"We were trying to figure out if you were a superhero."

I set the laundry basket down and got down on my knees to stare at these two precious faces.

"Oh my gosh, that sounds like serious business!" They both nodded, "What made you think about that?"

Seth still with a lisp and padded cheeks at 5 years old mustered up all his bravery,

"Momma! We think that you're a superhero and that you're not telling us. Like in that story that we read the other night."

My mind flashed back to our reading time when the boys were enthralled by the parents having super powers. I smiled and felt that very proud moment of feeling like *Damn, maybe I'm not such a failure as a mom afterall.* You know, dealing with all that typical mom guilt we get bombarded with every day with the ever-defeating mantra "You could be better! You could do more!" ridiculousness.

Caleb nodded passionately, "Yup. We really think you are." He leaned in and whispered, "And we think your superhero power is flying."

"Flying? Hmmm… Well, that is a great superpower isn't it?"

I tapped my chin, distracting them for a minute and giving me time to think of what direction to take this. I admit, I would probably most want *that* as my superpower if I had to choose. Either that or eating chocolate and drinking wine without getting fat and hungover. I might pick that one instead.

Seth agreed, "Yes. We keep checking to see if we have that super power, too, but when we look under our arms, we don't have those big flaps like you do. Do you think we'll get them when we get bigger so that we can learn to fly, too?" Caleb lifted my arm and wiggled the extra flab where my tricep used to be.

Seth smiled proudly at me while I gulped a big bunch of ego down the hatch.

Oh my lord. These children...

Not wanting them to feel bad for misinterpreting, I kissed them each on the cheek and said, "Well, how about we not tell anyone about mommy's superhero flaps and just keep it our little surprise."

"Can we tell, Daddy?" Caleb asked excitedly as I picked up the laundry basket to continue my superpower tasks.

I turned away from them and rolled my eyes, "Trust me, sweetheart, Daddy already knows."

Up until we watched "The Biggest Loser" together, they thought I was just a super hero.

And then, as my friends in England say, "The penny dropped."

Seth patted my tummy since his hand was already conveniently resting there while the computer rested on my legs.

"You should go on the show, Momma."

I turned to Thing 2 and said, "Believe it or not, even though I'm bigger than I'm designed to be, I'm actually the weight these people on the show are trying to get to. They'd be thrilled to be the weight that I am." I said as I closed the computer.

"Hey, it's not over!" They boys exclaimed.

"Ah, I think we've seen enough for one day. How about we make some gluten-free cookies?" They both cheered.

Another generation distracted by cookies.

I'm sure that's all going to work out just fine.

Oy vey.

––––––––––––––

In some ways...

I'm one of "those" people.

The people who don't have TV, shop at the health food stores and farmer's markets, and eat gluten-free and raw dairy,

And ask questions like,

"Is it organic? Better yet, it is pesticide-free?"

I drink green shakes and juice. And no, I'm not skinny but I have lost 80-something pounds after a weird year with a 100 pound weight gain (thyroid issues are so much fun).

Come to think of it, I've probably lost those 80 pounds a few times over, if you count carrying Thing 1 and Thing 2.

My husband says, "Stacey, I'm a healthier person just standing next to you with all those vitamins and supplements and the great way you feed our family. You really look out for us. I love that about you."

So, sweet. I'm not so sure that's a universal appreciation.

The other day when the gardener was walking by with his spray thingy in our townhome community, I stopped him and asked, "Hey Armando! What are you spraying there?"

He looked at the container and told me the name. It was poison. I don't know why they just don't call it "Poison" but then again, I do.

Because then, we'd act accordingly, but if you name it something pretty or powerful then, we bow to it instead of stand up to it.

The spray was one of those highly toxic things that make me crazy -- it's what some folks use to kill weeds instead of using something benign like vinegar or something. The guys are walking around in HAZMAT suits but I'm supposed to let my kids run around barefoot on the grass after they spray it.

No thank you very much.

My youngest son, Seth, turned to me after I told him not to go out in the greenbelt for a few hours, "Mom? Why don't they just pull the weeds instead of spraying poison on them for us all to breathe?"

He takes a gardening class at school where they use natural solutions to take care of pesky creatures.

He's nine.

I said, "Honey. Some people think that they're taking a short cut by spraying a poison instead of pulling the weeds."

I continued, "That company that makes the spray, also makes the genetically modified seeds I told you about."

He looked up at me. We've had some of these conversations before so, I kept going, "You know how God gave us the seeds freely to use and share? Well, there's a company that takes the seed, puts a poison pesticide inside to keep all the bugs away -- let's say in a tomato – and when they put the poison inside, they own the rights to the seed and can sell it for however much they want. They take the free gift from a generous God and make themselves a greedy god, and we have to pay for it with the poison inside of it."

I said, "Now, Seth if a bug won't even go near a food..."

He continued, "Don't eat it."

Seth asked, "Why don't they just plant marigolds around the tomatoes to keep the bugs away without needing to use all that bad stuff?"

Did I mention that he's nine?

I taught him that three years ago when we had a garden in our backyard.

When he was six.

Something I had learned from my Italian grandmother when I was his age.

I answered his "Why do people do that?" question:

"Because when we have the gifts of 'people' and 'money' here on earth and you begin to make money more important than people, you can lose your love for people and your wisdom about money."

"We gotta keep people first, Mom." Seth was convicted.

And even though I don't always hit the center of that target,

I agreed.

Talking with Seth got me thinking about what other places in life we've been given something freely and someone puts a poison in it.

I couldn't help but think of God.

You look all around and there's the beauty, abundance and regenerating power of nature. You see an endless universe, a solar system -- with all the planets, stars, moons and more than I can fathom to list -- all screaming evidence of a Force of creativity and generosity behind it.

I call it *God* but I also call it *Source, The Divine, The Spirit,*

and I call it *Love.*

So, here's this Love that has given us the capacity, inclination and ability to give and receive love.

A seed of love.

A seed that can be easily spread, thoughtfully nurtured, wisely protected, and can grow to do amazing things in our hearts and through our lives.

Its design is to nourish us and feed others. It gives us vitality and an ability to live the life of our dreams.

And at some point -- someone -- or a bunch of someone's, came together and took that free seed out of the wild and into the sterile lab of religion and placed a theology of fear inside the seed.

Poison.

They did it, espousing the same things that the GMO companies say, "It's to rid the world of the plight of hunger and save us from dying." But religions say, "We put the fear inside to rid the world of the plight of sin and to save us from eternal damnation."

And some people, who resonated with that particular mix of Love to Fear ratio consumed the seed. Oh, they didn't take it in because it was called "Fear" -- it was Fear masquerading as Love "If you do this, I'll love you. If you do that, I'll save you. If you believe in this, I'll bless you."

It's a very slippery slope. It has a lot of the appearances of love, but it doesn't resonate as Love.

Because it's not.

Calling Fear *Love* doesn't make it Love and the Divine in us knows it.

Like GMO seeds, the food that grows from them might please the taste buds but has less nutrition so, the body doesn't get what it needs and becomes weaker. It's harder to resist and easier to comply when you're weak. It's harder to think things through when you don't feel well and your brain isn't being fed the proper nutrition.

And in the places where people consume the Fear in a seed that was intended to be Pure Love, people get anxious, dependent, and unthinking -- they get weaker in their sense and trust of who they are.

Those "bugs" that wouldn't go near the GMO seed were the smart ones. Their instincts knew better.

Those atheists, agnostics, metaphysical, spiritual, non-religious folks wouldn't touch the food that the church grew from Fear.

We called them "crazy" and "sinners" and "unsaved" -- we weren't even able to recognize their health for staying away from our toxic thinking.

We in the church were calling their peace "a deception" while we called our anxiety "holy."

We called it the "Fear of God."

But God is Love.

And Love is pure.

Love does what Love is -- it Loves.

It's not in its nature to make us afraid of it.

We're supposed to be able to consume it, grow it, and feed others with it -- and we all live our dreams here on earth...

... *as it is in Heaven.*

I have conversations with my boys about Love. Not about sin.

When they were little, I used to ask them what the opposite of Up was, they'd say, "Down" and the opposite of High, they'd say, "Low." And the opposite of Love,

and they'd say, "Not Love."

Fear

is "Not Love."

Fear is GMO-Spirituality and I don't want to feed my kids that bullshit, non-nutritious poison.

Whether it's the poison inside a tomato seed, or the message on the television that says we're worth more if we look a certain way, or the fear that some churches put in their theology.

It's all indoctrination. Putting a crappy idea into someone's head is the emotional version of putting a crappy food inside of someone's body.

And if I feed that stuff to my kids, they may be able to consume some of it now in an innocent and trusting way because they're strong and pure -- but I know what it does to you in the long run. I've consumed foods and beliefs that were just tasty enough to be appealing but just damaging enough to unravel me. To recognize that is a painful gift.

I lived through enough of my own spiritual anxiety and mental self-hate because I consumed beliefs that became a dis-ease in my system. And I don't want to do that to my kids because that would be

"Not Love."

Love is Non-GMO Spirituality -- it loves to love us. It's a seed that grows and feeds our soul. It nourishes our lives and supports our dreams. It makes for happy people who hunger for wisdom and want to live in peace and cherish life.

I can ask myself 3 times a day:

What are you feeding your body?

But sometimes I need to stop and ask:

What are you feeding your soul...

16
A Veil of Fire

They worked together in the same office on the same floor of the World Trade Center -- didn't know each other's names, just the familiarity of their faces in the big accounting firm that serviced high-end clients from all over the world. Where they had previously nodded with courteous smiles, passing by the water cooler or Xerox copier, now they were locked eye-to-eye in terror as smoke, fire, and chaos surrounded them.

They found one open, working elevator, and jumped in with the throng of people eager to get out of the building that was having it's own version of Armageddon. They were the last ones to get in before the doors closed.

Standing side-by-side, breathless and terrified in the eerie silence surrounding, they all watched the floor numbers tick down, grateful to be escaping whatever hell was going on that they didn't fully understand. They would ask questions later -- now, they just needed to get out. The elevator went down almost 20 floors when it suddenly lurched to a stop and the doors slid open to a wall of fire, blazing in front of them.

Gasping screams came from inside the transport and the blinding noise of fire blared in front of them while one man pressed the "Close Doors" button with a fury -- as others were trying to physically grab the doors to pull them closed.

The man leaned to his female workmate and yelled close to her ear as the roaring fire approached, "We need to get out of here!" She motioned to the obvious threat in front of them. He nodded and explained quickly, "Sometimes, it's not all the way through -- it can be this veil of fire instead. Sometimes, there's oxygen on the other side. We need to try."

She nodded, knowing that these might be the last moments of her life either way, and took his hand that he was holding out to her. He counted and they threw themselves out of the metal box and into the fire, rolling on the ground as the elevator doors closed behind them.

He was right! They were beyond the flames! Both of them were burned all over, but adrenaline kept them focused as they crawled and then, ran to the stairwell and fled down from the 56th floor all the way to the bottom, taking the briefest pauses to collect some breath as their world was literally crashing down around them.

Finally out the doors, they collapsed in the care of the emergency workers who took them far away from the building and started treating their burns and wounds.

They later found out that everyone in the elevator had died.

These two strangers
Bonded forever
Survived
With scars and a story

Through the veil of fire.

It was one of the many stories on 9/11 that I have carried with me -- a day that took so much, brought so much, and taught so much. It was a day when I was supposed to be in Manhattan, preparing to sing in a building diagonal from the WTC, but I received a call 6 weeks prior and was placed in El Paso, Texas instead on that fateful day.

We lost our beloved priest from childhood, Father Mychal Judge, who left our parish to become a chaplain of the NYFD -- and who was the first victim of 9/11, pictured on the unforgettable Time Magazine cover as he was carried down the ashen streets by his devoted firefighters.

This story about the couple reminds me often, that we all have some kind of fire in front of us.

The thing we avoid
Because it's raging hot in threatening ways in front of us
So we lock ourselves in our elevators
Thinking we're safe
But we're really not.

When I went to a self-improvement course in 1995 and then, again, in 2007, I got present to my fire.

They call it your "story" - the conclusions you came up with based on three significant events that happened by the time you were 8 years-old.

It's the story with lots of different chapters,

Chapter 1: I'm Not Safe
Chapter 2: I Can't Trust
Chapter 3: If I Really Love Something, It Goes Aways
Chapter 4: I'm Unworthy of Good Things (Including Love, Faithfulness, Money, and Security)
Chapter 5: I Do Really Well "Under the Circumstances"
Chapter 6: I Create a Lot of Circumstances So I Can Do Really Well
Chapter 7: I Have to Control Everything Because I Can't Trust
Chapter 8: When I Let My Guard Down, Everything Falls Apart
Chapter 9: I Can Never Rest

And on and on

And on…

It's not a very good story.

I'm not in it all the time. I've done a lot of work "over the river and through the woods" to get to those places of freedom, but when I find myself triggered by the flames in front of me, I want to get into my little elevator and press the "close doors" button as fast as I can.

The unworthiness is probably the biggest punchline I've dealt with. The conclusions from the erratic inconsistencies in our home growing up -- and the abuse outside of it -- led to some disempowering chapters in my story. And, because I'm a really strong person, I can hold on for a long time, pretty tightly, to a bad idea.

My strength is both my super power and my kryptonite.

The stories show up as the obvious: running away from good stuff and avoiding what you don't feel you deserve. It can show up as choosing relationships that are distracting and take energy instead of giving it. And it can show up as sabotaging a good thing that's right in your midst.

Unworthiness, in particular, can also show up as its alter-ego, Entitlement.

We've all met that person who talks about how undeserving of something they are and then, act really expectant that life should be better than it is.

I had a friend, Carol, who illuminated that.

She was on a music team that I ran. She was fine as a group singer, but always thought she should get a solo. She'd tiptoe, in a subservient way, around the leadership like they were better than she was, and then, she'd sit and gripe about how incompetent they were to not choose her.

It was confusing.

I've done that myself in my marriage -- thinking I didn't deserve to be treated the way my husband was treating me, but at the same time, thinking I didn't deserve any better.

We have to do a whole lot of mental gymnastics to make our lives revolve around that kind of madness.

There was another friend in my life, my husband called her "Depressing Debbie" (even though that wasn't her name.) She'd come over and sit on my bed, literally crying and wailing about how she wanted to be married and felt like an old maid (at 22 years old):

"I DESERVE TO HAVE LOVE! I DESERVE TO BE MARRIED!!"

She did that for years. Over and over, until she got married in her late twenties.

Then, she'd come over and sit on my bed, crying and wailing, "I DON'T HAVE CHILDREN!!! I DESERVE TO HAVE CHILDREN!!"

My husband would roll his eyes as he walked by our bedroom door while I sat conflicted and comforting my friend. Conflicted, because I wanted to assure her in those good-girlfriend kinds of ways that, of course she deserved love (even though, honestly, I felt a little concerned for the dude who might show up on the doorstep of her craziness) but something just wasn't sitting right with me.

And it wasn't just Depressing Debbie's sentiments...

It was my clients who had gone through abuse, who sabotaged loving relationships in their lives.

It was friends who had weird theologies about God, who settled for so much less than life was offering them.

It was gifted men and women I knew in the community, who were walking around with their proverbial tails between their legs, in shame because of mistakes they had made during unenlightened times.

They all felt undeserving.

And that grated against my soul.

So, I turned it into a prayer in my journal, "Why does it bother me so much when I hear people say 'I deserve this or I don't deserve that?' Please help me understand why."

At some point, revelation came: the reason it bothered me was because *deserving* had an opposite:

If someone could be deserving, they could be undeserving.

Worthy could become unworthy.

Loveable could become unloveable.

And who gets to decide that? What subjective measure by the culture, the media, or some subjective person, who ate god-knows-what for breakfast, and hasn't had a good, healthy poop in god-knows-how long

Is deciding the fate of your worthiness for love, life, a spouse, children, money, and a dream trip to Aruba?

Who gets to decide if you're deserving or not?

It didn't seem right to me
Because it wasn't.

That's when this other word came strongly in the center of my thoughts:

"Design"

We're designed to love and be loved.

We're designed to grow and thrive.
We're designed to create and co-create.

We're simply designed that way.

It's not debatable
It's just what we do.

We do it all the time
Love. Grow. Thrive.

Every day.
From the time we're a baby to when we're a senior citizen. Whether we're an artist, or a teacher, or an architect.

It's not just what we do
It's who we are
Built right in the fabric of our being.

I started settling into that word 'design' for a few days, doing my stream of consciousness journaling around it, and I found myself really happy and settled there. Like I could rest.

And then, I realized why:

"Design" has no opposite.

You can't be undesigned.

You've already been created -- it's already been decided: once you're designed, you just get to live.

Once you're here, you're here. I mean, well, you're here until you're gone, but you know what I mean: you're not undesigned. No one erases you and starts over because you aren't good enough. You're here. Your footprint, energyprint, *soulprint* is forever in the universe.

The highest truth that I have considered and still resonates with me, is this:

There is some kind of God-Force, God-Source, Divine Intelligence, Great Spirit --
(Pick a word, any word -- make up your own word, be a poet -- it's all good.)

That Spirit is Inspired
That Force is Creative
That Source is Love.

So, if Love created us
From its Divine Inspiration
Then, that's what we're made of
So, we are Love, too
Here to Love and Be Loved.

It's not a question of worthy or deserving.

To me, it's about design.

And when I remember that -- my thick, consuming fires become veils.

I take action, instead of retreating back.

If I am designed for all the good things Love has planned
With all the good things Love has placed in me,
For all the good things Love has brought me here to do

Then, I am able to hold Truth's hand and jump through the thin stories of unworthiness
Of undeserving
Of shame and of doubt

And I soar, and roll and pat out the embers of the false beliefs that
are still burning
And run out the doors to freedom

To live the Love that I am designed to
Live in
And live out
In this great, big beautiful world

With this great
Big
Designed-And-Can't-Be-Undesigned

Beautiful

Me.

17
God is Bigger than the 'Nevers'

The doctor told us we would never have kids.

And that was

Just
Fine
With me.

I had heard enough horror stories about labor, toddlers, teenagers, and the tuition for college that made me really grateful to have the "Out of Operation" sign on my womb.

All good with yours truly.

In fact, I was so frustrated in my marriage that was struggling, and my health that was struggling that I stood on my front doorstep one day and told God, with my finger pointing toward the sky,

"You don't *ever* have to give me kids. I don't want them and I will *never* change my mind. Some people mature and change -- that won't be me, so thank you for giving me the gift of *not* being able to have kids."

I wagged my 26 year-old finger and all-knowing smugness at God.

(Let's all note that the prefrontal cortex in the brain -- the part that gives us an ability to make long-term decisions is not fully developed until we're about 27. Oy vey.)

I sounded like a brat.

A hurt brat -- because of where my marriage and health were -- but a brat, no less.

A few years later, I had been asked to lead music and speak at a conference in Hawaii. I never had an interest in going to Hawaii but my husband did. I had told him when we were first married, "Look, if someone calls us and says they want to pay our way, then, I'll go."

Got that call and off we went, my husband high-fiving God the whole way.

The first day of the conference went super well, beyond my expectations, but for some reason that night, I had a deep insecurity attack followed by a massive meltdown with God. I spent that night doing the ugly cry with snot running out of my nose under the big, Hawaiian moon. I finally reached the end of my tears, sniffled a few times, sighed, and eeked out a prayer, "God, would you show me your grace?"

And drifted off to sleep in my vulnerable, fragile state when this dreamy movie started playing in my head. It was me with a child in my arms -- a very ugly child. A baby so ugly, with a shock of black hair, that didn't even know what gender it was.

Despite all that, in my dream I was weeping uncontrollably over this child with such love.

I woke up with this bursting in my heart and leftover tears from my sleep saying, "Lord, I don't know if this means you're going to give me a child or if you're just letting me know you love me this much in my ugliness -- but whatever it is, let me never forget this feeling."

Two days later, some friends of ours flew out from California for their family vacation. We were all hiking in the Hawaiian waterfalls when the wife, Rebecca, turned to me and said, "Stacey! I had a dream two nights ago you were going to have a baby!" I turned and stared at her, "Rebecca! I had a dream two nights ago that I was holding my baby!"

Wow.

A few days later, we were at my favorite restaurant in Waikiki, "Eggs and Things" eating Macadamia nut pancakes with guava syrup. My lips were so happy, I could have done a hula dance right there.

There was a woman sitting at another table, who I had seen when we were all waiting to be seated. While we had been outside, I watched her interact with her grown daughter. I could see the kindness in the mother, but the daughter was so aloof, it was off-putting, even from the distance that I was observing them.

All during our breakfast, I felt magnetically drawn to the mother for some reason. I kept peeking her way and finally when she got up to leave, I leaned over to my husband whispered,

"I have to go talk to that lady."

He seemed confused, "Do you know her?"

"No." I answered, shaking my head.

He rolled his eyes in that, "What are you getting us into, Lucy??" kind of look that Ricky always gave her -- and then, he waved me on while he paid the bill.

I walked/ran to the woman I was now stalking outside of the restaurant and tapped her on the shoulder. She turned with a smile that said, "Hello" without saying a word.

"Ummm ... excuse me. You don't know me but, I feel like I'm supposed to talk to you. My name is Stacey and I do music and speaking around the country. Who are you?"

"My name's Pat." I heard the distinct twang in her voice, "And I'm a pastor's wife from Texas."

I smiled and said something I hadn't planned on saying, "Pat. I think you're supposed to pray for me." The words just fell out of my mouth as if someone else had put them there.

Well, she didn't pray for me, but her twenty-something daughter who I thought was rude and aloof, with big, blonde, Texas hair, lifted her hands high in the air and boomed with her loud Texas voice,

"DEAR LORD JESUS, WE LOVE YOU SO MUCH!!!."

And oh my god, I felt the people who were walking by us on the sidewalk just turn to stare. Then, my husband walked up to this little huddle and I felt his eyeballs nearly pop out of his head, staring at me. I couldn't even look at him for fear of turning into a pillar of salt.

I started praying really fast, too. Quietly. On the inside:

God, I am not embarrassed by you at all, but would you please lower her volume?

I couldn't even hear a word she was saying because I was so distracted by how loud she was and this deep desire for her to simply...

Shut
Up
Now.

That's when she lowered her voice and her hands to my belly and said, "And dear Lord, we thank you for this child. No, for these *children* you're going to give her. Lord, we thank you, now."

I hadn't said one thing to them about kids, infertility, or anything other than my name and what I did.

We left that place stunned.

Arriving back in California, more uncanny events unfolded:

In January, a friend called to say that she had a dream I was one month pregnant.
In February, a different friend called to say that she had a dream that I was two months pregnant.
In March, yet another friend had a dream that I was three months pregnant.

I said, "Oh my god, what's going on? Am I pregnant with being pregnant or something??"

I really wanted to deal with this physical issue of infertility and heard of a little healing center in a place called "Pleasant Valley Church" in Georgia. It was a place where I could go for two weeks to work on the mind, body, spirit connection.

So we did.

Oh my lord. I felt like I was in some alternate reality: Women in flower dresses from the 70's, with a splash of Laura Ingalls Wilder thrown in. It definitely didn't feel like the Southern California in 2001 that I had left just a few hours before.

It wasn't long before I set my judgments aside. This place was filled with kindness as they addressed matters-of-the-heart -- issues of unforgive-ness, fear and anger -- and they told story after story of people physically healed once these emotional/spiritual issues were resolved.

On the day when the topic was "Bitterness" they said, "We've noted in our work, that women who have conflict with other women tend to have issue of breast cancer, ovarian cancer, infertility..." I didn't hear whatever else they said after that.

But they said, "'infertility" and had my attention.

Geesh -- women in conflict with women...where do you even start with my Italian family of bossy Sicilians? It seemed like the men died early to get away from us and we were all in the kitchen making amazing meals and bitching at each other.

Truthfully, I went down the list and while I saw some relationships that could use some improvement and some unfinished places, there was no big, glaring, "AHA! NOW, I've got you!" kind of revelation.

I prayed for wisdom and went to sleep.

The next morning, I pulled a female pastor aside and said, "Donna, do you think that the woman I could be in conflict with -- is *me*?"

Her eyes were so warm with me, "Absolutely."

"Well, then that's what I admit: When I hear that God loves me, I have a hard time believing it. That's calling God a liar, which he's not. And, while I'm at it, I told God that I never wanted him to give me kids. Like ever. And that I'd never change my mind."

She nodded at my intense vow I had made.

"I want to take that back. I don't want to hold back any good thing from my life."

She smiled and agreed. We prayed a short simple prayer, taking back my vow and being willing to have the goodness of healing and children.

We went back to California that Spring after such a renewing experience. The pains in my abdomen that wracked me, stopped. The trips to the hospital that I had been making every other month for the five years prior for ovarian cysts, were no longer necessary.

I didn't know all of what was happening, but something had definitely changed.

That summer of 2001 was full of music and preparing for a busy Fall of traveling. I was especially excited about the month we were going to spend in the North East. I had conferences booked for State College, Manhattan, North Carolina and more. I was going to use that opportunity to see my family and go to my beloved San Gennaro's Feast in Little Italy in New York. Sausage and pepper sandwiches, huge blocks of Torrone candy, and hot and cold running cannoli.

Being Italian, I'm pretty sure, if you sliced me open, you'd find cannoli filling -- and a few thousand meatballs.

The feast was pretty much my idea of heaven and a tradition for my family when I grew up in New Jersey. I hadn't been in years and even though it was only July, I was smacking my lips in anticipation of September.

When one day, the phone rang. I picked up the imitation retro phone that weighed about a thousand pounds, sitting on the desk in the downstairs office of our townhome.

"Stacey? It's Peter." It was my conference coordinator calling from LA. He was a transplant from Boston and I would know his voice anywhere.

"Hey Peter, how are you? I'm looking forward to seeing you next month in Portland."

"Yes, me, too Stacey…" He paused, "I just wanted to let you know as soon as I did that we need to switch you off of Manhattan in September."

I furrowed my brow to Rock who had just walked into the office, "Why? What happened?"

Peter said, "Jamie's coming out from England on holiday with his family for six weeks and since he'll be out here, he wants to do New York."

Jamie was a great guy and since he had started the program, he definitely had seniority.

"Are you sure, Peter? I have all those other events in the Northeast and was planning on being there the whole month." I was trying to not sound desperate even though I was so disappointed.

"I'm happy to trade Jamie my Hawaii in January for Manhattan in September."

I heard Peter's resolve, "I'm sorry, Stacey. This is just the way it is. We've switched you and Rock to El Paso for that September week instead and then, you can fly out for the rest of the East Coast dates."

El Paso, Texas? Good lord -- I'm giving up the panache of New York City for the dry, dusty heat of Western Texas. What a thrill.

Not.

I sighed a disappointed sigh, "Okay, Peter. You got it."

After I hung up and gave Rock the full scoop, he said to me, "Come on! Put your Italian on! Call back and try again. You're very persuasive -- go be persuasive."

I went to put my hand on the old-style phone and it was like someone was holding it back from dialing.

I looked up at my husband, "I'm not supposed to Rock. I know this is going to sound weird, but I feel like this is for me. I'm just going to let it go."

———————

A few weeks later we were up in Portland standing at the airport waiting for our flight back to Orange County after another successful conference. That deeply satisfied feeling was mixed with some distraction.

I stood by the window of Southwest Airlines, watching the planes take off and land. It was something my dad used to do when he went through a rare time of fear in his many travels. He would count the planes landing and taking off in a five minute period and then, multiply that by all the airports in the world and find himself comforted by the numbers of safe flights.

While I didn't feel afraid that day, I didn't have total peace.

Rock came to stand beside me with his cup of airport coffee when I turned to him with a serious look and said these words spontaneously, "There's going to be a tragedy in the air in America. There's going to be a tragedy in the air in America. There's going to be a tragedy in the air in America." He looked at me, confused and concerned. "It's going to be awful." I closed my eyes and shook my head and then, looked at him again, "It's going to be terrible, Rock."

"What? How? What do you think we're supposed to do??"

I shook my head and breathed deeply, searching his eyes with mine, "I think we should just pray and send an email to others on our team to pray." We had teammates all over the world, traveling every week throughout most of the year.

Rock and I soberly tucked our travel bag under our seats, secured our buckles and held hands to pray our usual prayer of "God send angels around us."

But this time when we prayed, Rock squeezed my hand, "What did you just say??" He asked with intensity.

"I don't know what you're talking about. What did I say?"

It was like I was in a haze.

"You said, 'I pray against a spirit of terrorism' -- why would you say that?"

I shook my head back and forth, "I don't know. I don't even remember saying that."

We flew with a tension that we both could feel. We were restless and upset but didn't really understand why.

When the plane landed back in Orange County, we felt relieved but something was still restless.

We were quiet on the way home.

———————

My legs were in the stirrups for that yearly event of my female check-up. The two things that made it palatable was that my husband was beside me, feeling just as uncomfortable as I was, and one of my dearest friends had been my gynecologist for the last 15 years doing all the awkward exploration around my female bits.

She snapped off her rubber gloves and covered my knees with the paper drape.

I sat up for the report, "Stacey, the pregnancy test came back negative."

Rock and I were both sober as she continued, "It's been 13 years for you guys, right?"

I answered, "Well, we've been married for 13 years but we haven't been trying that long."

Stephanie knew of our trip a few months prior to the healing place in Georgia and I had shared with her about the amazing dream and confirmations in Hawaii that happened a few months before that.

She nodded and placed a loving hand on my arm, catching Rock's eyes so he could see her compassion before she turned back to me, "I really think it's time we try some intervention to help you guys out."

We knew this was an option but we had never said it out loud before. Stephanie continued talking as she turned to her desk drawer and started putting things into a white paper bag. She leaned over and wrote something on her prescription pad and grabbed something else from the drawer.

"Stacey, Rocky -- you are going to be wonderful parents one day and these may help that to happen sooner. I want you to start taking these prenatal vitamins." She handed me the bag.

"And fill this prescription to help you ovulate more consistently." She handed me the prescription.

"...And call him," She pointed to the name on the card, "he's one of the best in the field -- if I had a daughter, I would send her to him."

I nodded, still not able to find my words, while she leaned over with all her Greek Orthodox love and kissed me on both cheeks that now had tears rolling down my face.

Rock waited silently while I got dressed. We checked out and walked down to the parking lot.

I touched his arm and he stopped. I looked my husband in the eyes and said, "Honey. I love you. I believe we're supposed to have a kiddo, but I just don't want to do it this way. We've gone through so much. I don't want to stand on my head to get pregnant, or turn our bedroom into a circus. Then, sex turns to stress and that's not gonna get me pregnant any faster to have all that pressure so..."

I handed him the bag, with the prescription and card in it and said, "...I just think if God wants us to have a baby, we're going to have a baby. Right now, this is my peace."

I let him hold on to the bag while I held onto my faith.

We didn't have a lot of time to focus on that, because we had events to perform all weekend before flying out to the illustrious El Paso, Texas.

Woo-hoo.

I don't normally drink on a flight -- not for any moral reasons -- it's just because I hate using the bathroom on a plane so, I essentially dehydrate myself on a trip and then, guzzle a bunch of water and a sizeable glass of wine when we land.

This flight to El Paso was different. It was short, only two hours, but I drank two strong Bloody Mary's while we were en route.

That restlessness I felt in July was more intense lately. I couldn't shake it. It had that feeling like when you turn a jack-in-the-box: the song gets more frantic as the box about to pop open.

I felt myself winding up and the frantic feeling was increasing.

We landed and were transported to the hotel. I just wanted to go to bed and make this feeling go away.

Monday morning I woke up and felt worse. I turned to Rock on the way to breakfast, "I'm not eating today. I feel like I should fast and pray about this awful feeling inside of me. I don't know what's going on but I can't shake this."

He put his hand on my back, "Honey, you're going to be on and off stage for 14 hours today. You need your energy."

I turned to him, "I need my peace. This is awful."

The day was bumpy. It's not usually like that. We met with the hosts of the event that night, while they sat eating pork fajitas and I sat in front of an empty plate. They admitted that they felt off, too.

In bed that night, my sleep was fitful. Tossing, turning, until I woke up at 2:30 a.m., writhing in emotional pain. I was that way for 2 hours not knowing what to say to God, until I finally just selfishly begged, "Please just let me go to sleep. I haven't eaten and I have a full day ahead. Please, just have some mercy and let me rest."

Two hours later, I went to sleep.

The alarm went off at 6:15. We stirred, our bodies all tangled up and we found ourselves making love out of both distraction and pleasure.

I heard my own voice inside of me say, "I just got pregnant." And this smile came over my whole being. I just knew that I knew that I had a baby inside of me.

With no time to catch the morning news, we hopped in the shower, grabbed our music and ran to the elevator, my sweet secret inside of me, distracting me for a moment.

But only for a moment. The minute the elevator doors opened, we saw a lobby full of people with distraught faces turning to the large TV high on the wall.

We turned in time to see the second plane flying into the Twin Towers in Manhattan.

Diagonal from the building where my team was preparing for the New York conference.

The place where I was originally supposed to be.

The days that followed were surreal. Stranded in Texas watching the news of the unimaginable in New York. My family priest growing up in New Jersey, who had become a chaplain for the NYFD, was the first victim of 9/11, and our entire team was forced down into the basement across from the WTC, covered in soot. We were so relieved to hear from them 24 hours after everything, literally, collapsed.

A woman approached us and asked, "Do you need a car to get back to California? My son lives there and I have an extra car you can take."

We drove in mostly silence and tears as the unreasonably quiet, blue sky loomed overhead. It felt like it should just rain every day after such a massive tragedy.

But it didn't.

And it didn't seem fair that life should go on.

But it did.

I got back to California and found out that yes, indeed, I had gotten pregnant on that morning of 9/11. The life inside of me was finding a way, against so many odds, to be here on this side of the world.

Little did I know how much that strong, determined, resilient spirit would show itself in so many ways in his life and in mine, reminding me that the "Yes" inside of Caleb was so much bigger than the doctors who said I'd never have kids, or the part of me that never wanted to.

I definitely don't understand why I heard these messages, had these dreams, or felt this restlessness. I can't draw definitive conclusions in one direction or another. I drew a lot of conclusions during my crazy religious times, when I was coming more from judgment than I was from love. Now, I'm just more comfortable with the "I don't knows" and blank spaces. All I know is it happened. I'm not even sure I did all that I could in the circumstances, but I did what I did, and the result was what it was.

I just know this:

That every time I hear a client who tells me that the doctor said they'll never get better
Or I meet a woman who thinks she'll never get married
Or I talk to a kid who says that they'll never make the play they're auditioning for

I hear this little voice inside me say,

God is a "Yes" who's totally available to us
And that God -- that Divine "Yes" -- is bigger than the "nevers."

18
The Power of Hormones

It was the day after my first son was born.
Which was a week after my contractions had started.

One week.
Contractions between 4-10 minutes apart for 5 of those unforgettable 7 days.

To say that I was exhausted was the understatement of the century.

After close to 60 hours of labor, Caleb was born.

If I hadn't worked so hard to get him out, I would have given him such a pinch.

Oy vey.

My friend, Jackie, was by my side the minute he was on the outside. Loving on Caleb and me and telling me what a good job I had done. Her family was like family to me and her daughter, Meredith, had been one of my favorite voice students for years when I had been teaching.

After all the post-birth "Ooh's" and "Ahhs", Jackie left and said she'd be by later with Meredith to see the baby that we had all courted for the last 40 weeks.

So, mid-day that first day, I stirred awake from some sleep and looked over to see Jackie and Meredith sitting there beside my hospital bed.

"We were just about to leave," Jackie said, "you were sleeping so soundly." I reached out my hand and let out a creaky, "No, stay." and pointed to the tray with the cranberry and 7-up spritzer that quenched my thirst and gave me a wild case of the toots.

I scooched myself up, took a deep sip, and realized I was sweating. So hot. Couldn't get cool. It was like I was sitting inside of a hairdryer.

When I looked up at the vent above me, blowing fiercely on my head, I said to Jackie,

"Oh my god," I tried to block the air with my hands, "why do they have the heat on in June??"

I threw off the sheets and started fanning myself with my lunch menu.

Jackie smiled, "Oh honey, that's not the heat, that's the air conditioning. Welcome to your hormones."

Oh. my. Lord.

Jackie got me a wet washcloth to help me cool off. I truly thought she was messing with me so, when the nurse came a few minutes later with Caleb in her arms, I asked her. She said the same thing as Jackie, only in her own sassy, nurse-y way, "It's like a refrigerator in here. It's just your hormones losing their mind."

I rolled my eyes, took my baby who had more hair than Elvis, and looked playfully in his deep blue eyes.

I love you, you little stinker. Epic labor, stretch marks, cellulite and now this.

You better be really good in your teenage years because, I'm gonna need it if these hormones keep playing with my head like this.

Caleb looked in my eyes, and blinked at me with a serious look.

I'm pretty sure we had a deal.

Hormones aren't the only thing that make you feel like up is down, in is out, and hot is cold.

Life can do that too.

Well, actually, the stories that we make up about life.

You know, those running narratives in our head -- where we've made up stuff because of something bad that happened and then, we live in relationship to the story in our head instead of the actual reality that's in our midst.

I spent so much of my life, living in the stories that didn't serve me or my heart
That shredded my confidence
And made me feel like I didn't belong.

Stories can make you feel the opposite of what is true.

That you're unlovely
When you're really lovely.

That your unholy
When you're really holy.

That you're unworthy

When you're really worthy.

And on
And on
And on.
I'm not really sure which event was my big undoing or if it was a series of events that sent a strong message that I eventually grabbed onto while it was unraveling me.

When I went to a humanistic class for a few years I was in search of answers.

The philosophy of the class stated that we had three main events that occurred by the time we're 8 years-old that define our sense of who we are. That we spend a lifetime operating from the belief we form at that time.

It's a compelling thought.

So, if it's atmosphere, culture, religion, events -- nature vs. nurture -- or likely some combination of all of them with a dash of destiny, fate and whatever else thrown in, we end up with some stories and ideas about who we are and what life is.

I remember my elementary school principal. He had a long name that started with an "L" and ended with "camp" or something like that. All I remember is that we called him "Mr. Lollipop" because that pretty much described his shape. It's one thing to see an overweight person, and it's another to see a round person. And, whether my memory serves me correctly or not, the thing that I remember about Mr. Lollipop was that he was round.

Well, he walked in one day to our 5th grade class. I was still new to the school and finding my way after that big move up to the New Jersey mountain area -- and away from the city where everything was a walk or quick bike ride away. This was more isolating and I felt more alone. Mr. Lollipop was doing his rounds, as he did once a week or so, to check in on the classrooms and make his presence known. He'd stop at a desk or two and look at a student's work and then, move on to another room.

We all got so excited when he came in -- nervous really -- the teacher's voice changed slightly and we all sat up a little taller, and got a little more quiet in our chairs. Mr. Lollipop walked up one row and then, turned to walk down my row. I heard him behind me and then, within a moment he was next to me. Right beside my desk and standing on my foot, which I didn't realize was peeking out from under my desk.

Oh my lord. I stopped breathing. He was not a light man and I was torn! Do I say something or do I just pretend that everything's fine?? I couldn't even think straight about making my handwriting neat or the work I was doing. Some of the kids around noticed that his foot was on top of mine and started giggling. Mr. L turned his head quickly toward me with a frown -- as if I had done something behind his back to make them laugh. I hadn't. But it was too late and I didn't know how to explain. He walked away, off of my foot -- bringing me both relief and anguish. Now he didn't think well of me.

I hate when people don't think well of me.

Later on that day, I was walking down the school corridor -- I had gotten a pass to stay later in a class and the hallways were empty while everyone was settled in their next class. Empty, except for me and and someone walking down the hall in my direction. It was Mr. Lollipop! He was moving toward me and I was moving toward him. I clutched my books to my chest where my heart was pounding with fear and I smiled as big a smile as I could, "Hello, Mr. L! How are you?"

He looked right past me and kept going.

Oh my god. It's me. He doesn't like me. He hates me... my life is ruined.

(Because you know, that's what you think when you're in 5th grade and you have some of those people pleasing things going on inside of you and you have authority, father-issues and "I wish I could disappear" issues.)
I spent the next year and a half that we lived there thinking that the man hated me. And not only that, years beyond that -- until I was in my 20's. Out of all the memories from living there those two years, that one stood out the most.

It wasn't until I went to that self-development class in my 20's that I realized that I had made that event mean something. That my memories were what they were because of the story I had told myself that day when he stepped on my foot in class and stepped right past me in the hall.

I had concluded he didn't like me, thought I was a bad kid, and labeled me in that category and didn't see me as a good student, a good kid, or a respectful person.

When I realized that I was the one who had come to those conclusions, I realized that I had the power to change that. Maybe he walked past me quickly because he had gas, or diarrhea and had to get to the bathroom in his office quickly. Maybe there was an emergency phone call, or a kid who was sick, or maybe the Superintendent of schools had come by for an unexpected visit.

The truth? I didn't know. But in my not-knowing, I had filled in the blanks of "He doesn't like me and he thinks I'm a bad kid."

The reason that matters is because I reacted to my conclusions as if they were true. I tried to overcompensate and prove myself -- because I thought he didn't like me. I brought gifts and apples to his desk, because I thought he didn't like me. I tried to say nice things about him, really loud within earshot around him, because I thought he didn't like me.

I changed me -- and my natural actions and reactions to things, all because I thought he didn't like me.

That's a mild example in my life.

And maybe for yours, too.

———————

I spent years thinking I was unworthy of love because I had gone through sexual abuse. I thought I was ruined -- and acted ruined and made choices based on the thoughts that I was already ruined (so why not drink and do other destructive things anyway…).

When my husband wouldn't stand up for me or protect me, I thought it meant that I wasn't valuable enough (a result of being 'ruined'). So, I felt less-than and like I needed to prove myself as valuable. I spent years spinning my wheels and overworking in my career, just to prove to people that I was valuable by earning my keep.

I made myself sick in the process.

The stories don't tell us the truth. They tell us the opposite. Like the hormones did that day that I had given birth.

What seemed hot was cold. It really felt that way to me. And it was my truth -- I truly did feel hot -- but it wasn't the whole truth -- because the truth was the cold air was blowing -- it's just that it wasn't registering for me. My body was in a state where it's system was off and what was real and true wasn't coming off as that.

My journey has been learning about how to separate the two: The "this is how I feel" from the "this is what's really going on" kind of stuff. I don't always have it sorted out. It's messy to process and sticky to separate. Our feelings want to tell us that they're right. But if they're not based on the truth, then we're spending a lot of our time wallowing over twisted illusions.

The things that you're going through -- whether it's the health crisis or the marriage issue or the financial bump -- none of those things mean anything about you at your core. You're still wonderful. You're still amazing. You're still here with a great purpose. The problem comes when we tie what's going on, with how we feel, and we draw a conclusion about it all -- and then, live as if that conclusion is the whole truth -- when it's not.

Because I know that I don't always have the clearest read, I ask questions. Byron Katie, creator of "The Work" has excellent ones, "Is this true?" is my favorite one to start with.

Like when one of my coaching clients came to me with her husband's affair. She had concluded that, because he cheated on her, she wasn't beautiful anymore.

I asked, "Is it true?"

She answered, "That he cheated on me? Yes!"

I said, "No. The other part."

"Oh…" She was quiet for a second, "That I'm not beautiful? Well, I feel not beautiful. I feel discarded and unimportant. Like I was trash. He treated me like trash and I feel ugly."

I nodded. That made sense that she felt so awful. But her conclusions weren't accurate. She was beautiful and she was hurt. But she was living as if she wasn't beautiful. She had surgery scheduled to correct what she thought was wrong with her and even though that was her choice to make, I didn't want her making it from a false understanding of herself.

It took time for her to see and understand that one part was real and true (he cheated) but the other part, the conclusion she was coming to about herself was a default setting of hers. She could have come up with other conclusions like,

"He's an ass."
"It's good for me to know so that I can be free."
Or, "He doesn't value a faithful wife like me."
Or, "Wow, that was really an unwise move."
Or something more neutral.

Her conclusion was not accurate and it was destructive to her.

I loved the movie "A Beautiful Mind" with Russell Crowe. (Spoiler Alert) It's a real-life story where Crowe plays John Nash, a brilliant mathematician and cryptographer who was also antisocial. He saw apparitions and engaged them as if they were real because he truly thought they were. Some of their input was destructive to not only his peace of mind but to his marriage and child. His imagination world of false beings was tearing at his sanity. At some point, Nash realized that he was aging and the apparitions were not. It was the proof he needed to see that they weren't real. Nash realized that he didn't have a handle on what was truth and what wasn't. Part of being restored to his wife and child -- and his sanity -- were finding ways to decipher reality from imagination.

At some point near the end of the movie -- after Nash has recaptured his life and is teaching at a university -- a man who he doesn't recognizes approaches. Nash turns to his students and asks, "Is there a man standing there? With white hair and a pen in his pocket." The puzzled students smile and answer, "Yes." And then, Nash engages the stranger.

He found a way to assess what was reality, and what wasn't, by asking questions from sources he knew that he could trust.

The funny thing was this: The apparitions didn't go away, but as he had reconciled them in his mind as not telling him the truth, they stopped talking to him. The constant input and goading was gone. They were silent and the inner torment ceased.

Pilots are a great reminder of this to me: When they're in a storm and lose their sense of their position -- an experience called "Spatial Disorientation" happens and they have to look at the instruments instead of looking at the horizon or trusting their feelings. In the tossing of the storm -- and the fatigue of it all -- they can lose their sense of where they are and if they're upside down or not. Too many pilots have lost their lives by thinking that what they saw out the window and how they felt was the whole story, when it wasn't. The instrument was the truth-teller and could keep them flying upright when they were getting off course..

We all have those times -- those times where we draw conclusions on our feelings -- and our internal stories -- instead of acting on the truth.

Some people refer to it as "Little 't' Truth" and "Big 'T' Truth. The things that feel or seem real -- our little "t"s (how we feel) do best when bowing to the Big "T" Truth of what is real.

It's a process to see life for what it is.

Sometimes it takes running into the same wall of misbelief a thousand times and saying, "Wow. That actually hurts. I think I'll stop doing that."

Sometimes it takes creating some litmus tests to measure things by. I wrote about it in my Bloom Beautiful book:

You know how the saying goes "The truth shall set you free."
So, here's the deal:
If you're making assessments of yourself,
"I'm unworthy."
"I'm unlovable."
"I'm undeserving."

And you're not wildly freed by those thoughts
Then, it's gotta be that they're
Just
Not
True.

Like me with Mr. Lollipop
Or about the size of my hips
Or the past abuse.

I wasn't free when I made presumptions based on circumstances. They tied me up in knots and changed the way I lived. Relationships suffocate in a place of presumption. I've killed a few in my day.

On that hot, post-labor moment, the cold air was blowing, but I felt so hot. Can you imagine what it would have been like if I ran through the hospital with my butt sticking out of the gown, blaming the nurses and orderlies for putting the heat on in June? That wouldn't have gone over so well. My presumptions and lack of asking questions, would have me acting on the wrong conclusions. But because my friend helped me understand that my hormones were going wonky and that I wasn't getting an accurate read, I could ask for something to cool me off and some tips to support my hormones while they were riding the rollercoaster.

See how non-drama that is and how much easier it is to navigate the harder parts of life when we don't add on something else?

Our stories can make us feel like life is upside down when we're really right side up.

Thankful for the friends
And the instruments
The self-development classes
and the key questions

that help us to get back to the truth --

so that the truth can set us free.

19
The Road Trip from Hell

We were doing it. We were leaving our home of Southern California and heading cross-country to a little village in the Northeast. It housed 2 prisons, 7 churches, and 2,500 people. Our job assignment for the next couple of years was going to be about bringing spiritual and practical encouragement to the community along the Hudson River. We would do that through our music, speaking and just being a growing family in the midst of families who were needing some support.

Moving from Southern California -- the land of beautiful sunsets, perky boobs, and eternal youth, to the quaint, quirky village in Upstate New York -- was going to be a culture shock for my family but, I was ready. I loved the West Coast so much but felt eager for a change to a quieter, more spacious location and to share something from my East Coast upbringing with my native Californian husband and two small boys.

People asked us all the time, "How did you end up in Upstate New York and why the heck would you ever leave Southern California?"

One afternoon, on October 29th, 2004, a hat interrupted the rhythms of our life.

We were standing in Nordstrom Rack at a rare day off together. It was the "poor man's" version of the regular Nordstrom (if "poor" meant that you made 100k a year and didn't want to spend half of that on a suit) and my go-to place when I have to grab a pair of shoes that aren't going to cost me a scrillion dollars.

Caleb and his new little brother, Seth, were being watched for a few hours in between Seth's feedings. I had just enough time to grab a coffee and a trip to Metro Pointe South where the store was, before I sported two wet, embarrassing rings on the front of my blouse.

"Hey! Check this out!" I said, trying on this adorable black and grey leopard, fuzzy winter hat. It was a warm October day -- our hottest month of the year -- 85 degrees and sunny outside with the dry Santa Ana winds blowing from over the mountains.

Rock rolled his eyes with that *I thought we were here for shoes* look. "God, you're making me sweat just looking at you." He felt my forehead, "You feeling alright?"

"Oh, I'm fine!" I twirled to the side to look at my reflection from another angle and tugged on the sides of the brim, "This is my 'East Coast in January' hat!" I exclaimed.

He looked confused, "Do you know something I don't know?"

I shrugged, "I think we're going to go to the East Coast for the month of January to do our music and speaking."

He had that Ricky talking to Lucy voice, "Okaayyy… have you prayed about it?"

I said, "Nope."

I took the hat off of my head and handed it to him. He looked at me with a raised eyebrow and said, "Pray about it."

I nodded and put my hand to my head in a salute.

Totally forgot to pray about it.

Didn't even really think about it until, a few days later, on Halloween, we received an e-mail from a female priest I had worked with years before, but hadn't been in touch with for at least a year: "Stacey, I know that you are in California but I wanted to reach out and make a request: In prayer, I felt the Holy Spirit leading me to invite you out to the little church I'm moving to in Upstate New York. I'm being ordained to this new parish in January and thought you could come out for the month to do music for our church, my ordination, and for the community at large."

I read the e-mail to Rock who was standing there with his jaw hanging open.

"Welp," he closed his mouth and swallowed hard, "I guess we're going to be on the East Coast in January, just like you said." His voice trailed off as he turned to walk down the hallway towards the boys' room.

I whispered under my breath as I peeked at the Nordstrom bag in the corner,

"Good thing I bought the hat."

If you know anything about January of 2005, it was the coldest winter that the East Coast had seen in 20 years.

Both boys got the flu while we were snowed in on the top floor of a Victorian rental unit, and my 2 ½ year-old, who wouldn't hold anything down, started nursing again. So, now I had two kiddos hanging off my boobs while we were trying to be flexible with the weather, and get the work done that we came to do.

My native California husband would watch the news report, "Today's high will be 11 degrees." He'd turn and give me a deadpan look, "Eleven," he'd say dryly, "is not a 'high.'"

Flip flops, cut offs and surf boards just weren't going to be very useful here.

But, despite all the storms and signs that we should run, screaming back home, something was drawing me. I felt like we were supposed to be there.

"My heart feels at home here, Rock"

I swear, I heard him hate me.

My husband shook his head, vehemently, "Nuh uh. No way, babe. Not now -- not ever. It would take a sign from *God* to get me to move here, Sta."

I raised my eyebrows and kinda knew he was done for.

Apparently, he got whatever sign he needed, because when we came back to California the word was out: The Robbins' family was moving to New York.

———

With an infant and toddler "helping", packing took on the form of a circus act.

Kids climbing in boxes, out of boxes, pooping in boxes -- all of that was crazy enough but then, I was trying to work and wrap up our life before moving 3,000 miles away.

All I wanted to do was get the truck packed and on its way, while our family climbed into the van for some quality time together.

My friends kept asking me,

"Are you *sure* you want to drive *all* the way?
With the *kids*?
In the *van*?"

What? Was I going to strap them to the roof or leave them somewhere?

Of course we were driving. It was going to be great!

How could it not? I had blank journals, healthy snacks and parenting books on CD. It was going to be a bonding time for our family -- a time to get reacquainted to each other after such a big push and so many teary farewells.

I imagined us writing our work goals in the blank journals before we arrived in New York. I dreamed of stopping at state parks for our lunches while the children frolicked in the nature under their feet, and I envisioned the kids napping in the car while my husband and I held hands and listened to parenting CDs so that we could become extraordinary parents as we drove three thousand miles across the US.

With two kids in diapers.

Across the whole freakin' country.

At what point did I lose my mind and think that this was a good idea?

What
Was I thinking?

I mean, how did I forget that my kids cry on the 10 minute trip to

Trader Joe's down the street from my home. How were they going to make it across 15 states?

And that my husband -- *oh my lord* -- has magnetic attraction to MacDonald's hamburgers the minute he hears the words "road trip."

Or that my bladder only holds about 17 miles, if I'm lucky, since having Thing 2 do his gymnastics routine in my belly...

Oh no.

What was I thinking?

What did I do...

We hit every weird weather system imaginable: Torrential rains in California, a monsoon in Arizona, and hail the size of softballs in New Mexico. We went in the wrong direction for hours (more than once) and ended up driving an average of 250 miles a day. I had only planned for a six-day trip.

At the rate we were going, it would take two weeks.

We're not going to make it if it takes that long, I told myself. *My will to live isn't strong enough.*

Juice spilled on the journals. We lived at McDonalds. No one pooped. No one slept. Everyone cried at some point, including my husband. The cellophane never made it off of the parenting CDs.

This was so very not good.

By day 4, we reached El Paso. I had *had* it. I was ready to ship the little people and the big person off in FedEx boxes to the East while I had my own Thelma and Louise experience off the edge of the great state of Texas.

At one point, I thought we should just give up, stay in Western Texas and live there. We were never going to make it to New York

Alive.

It was the road trip from hell.

By Day 8 of our 6-day road trip, we crossed into Pennsylvania. I could have cried but I was too exhausted.

We drove and drove, and then drove some more. Pennsylvania is the East Coast's version of Texas: You can drive for forever and a day and still be in the same state.

It's pretty and picturesque, but, at some point, it's aggravating.

The good thing about our trip was that it was easy to find a hotel: Every day I'd open my trusty AAA guide, make a call and we'd have a place in about 10 minutes. It was one of the only graces I could see on this journey, other than my husband not cutting me up into tiny pieces and leaving me in a bag on the side of the road for getting us into this mess.

That last day in Pennsylvania felt like an eternity and unlike the ease we had all the other days, on this one we could not find a place to stay. Business conferences, military conventions and a televangelist-palooza meant that the rooms were either booked or a ridiculous rate of $250 a night.

"I am not paying $250 a night to *not* sleep." I declared to the everyone and no one listening in my car.

Finally, after 12 hours we called and found the one hotel for 75 bucks in the business district of Harrisburg. The rain was pouring and had been all day, and the trucks were merciless, flying by at reckless speeds on harrowing turns. With two kids who fell asleep in their car seats without any dinner and my husband napping in the passenger seat, I was determined to get us there and redeem this freakin' awful nightmare of a situation.

As I went to take our off-ramp, I put on my right blinker just in time for an 18-wheeler to get between the exit and me and I missed the one place I could get off. I had to drive around the city, lost and exhausted for another 45 minutes.

That was it. I was done.

Life - 17 million, Stacey - 0.

You win.

Clenching the steering wheel, with tears down my face, I could barely breathe out the words,

"Why, God, *why*??? *Why* is this happening to us when we're trying to go to New York to do GOOD things! I mean, really, do people who are plotting crimes and mass destruction get this many obstacles?? *What* is going on? *Why* is this happening? I'm going to help people in need and I'M the one who's going to need to be *institutionalized* before we get to New York. You have to help me. I am not normally a "why" person, but right now? I just need to know *why*..."

I was a whimpering mess by the time we pulled into the hotel.

The kids were awake and I had no dinner for them and no plans to get in the car again. The restaurant had closed and room service had ended for the night.

Oh good, just shoot me.

Spying some bananas on the counter, I slipped a bunch through my fingers and took two kids, a resentful husband, and all of our luggage up to the room.

After jumping on the beds for an hour (the kids, not me) I laid us all down and prayed the same prayer just one more time:

This is so hard, God. I just need to know why...

Day 9 and the sun was shining. Finally. It was one of the first sunny days on our entire trip and the last day of travel. I turned to my wide-awake almost 2 ½ year-old and said, "You love pancakes, Caleb." His eyes grew wide and he nodded with excitement, "And we're not eating one more hotel, lobby bar breakfast. (I personally couldn't face one more hard-boiled egg with a side of raging constipation). So, let's go find pancakes, honey!" We cheered and high-fived while Caleb ran around the room like a race car. I turned to my husband and said, "We'll meet you and Seth downstairs." He nodded wearily as Caleb and I took off.

As I was getting directions to the nearest diner from the concierge, Caleb wandered away from me into the hotel lobby where the breakfast was served. He must have been on automatic pilot.

The next sound I heard were the screams. Top of the lungs, top of the morning, "somebody-hurt-me-or-somebody-pissed-me-off" kind of screaming. It was Caleb and I went running.

I found him sobbing under a countertop that was filled with coffee pots and tea kettles.

"Honey, are you okay? What's wrong, Cay?" I was scanning his body, patting down his limbs and belly, searching for the owie.

"Oh, he's fine!" A short, perky woman who had a slight Peter Pan vibe and glimmer in her eye appeared next to us. She had obviously slept more than I had and was trying to assure me.

"He just tried to touch the coffee pot but I told him, 'No' and he got scared."

I sighed with relief while comforting my son and "Uh-huh-ing" her.

"He's so cute, how old is he?"

"Two and a half," I said, distractedly.

"Oh! I have a 2 ½ year old grandson!"

I nodded while she continued,

"What's his name?" she asked.

"Caleb." I answered.

"Oh! My grandson's name is Jackson and I bet they would get along great."

At that point, she could have told me her grandson was Michael Jackson and she was Princess Amidala and

I
Wouldn't
Care.

I didn't have enough energy to care about my own life, let alone hers and *plus*, she was irritating me with how "up" she was. I started praying, *Please, just make it all stop and go away. Please - if you're a God of compassion -- make <u>her</u> stop and go away.*

I looked haggard. No make-up. No shower. No sleep. And the daily diet of highly nutritious Big Macs, along with wrong turns and kids screaming, had finally taken it's toll. I had officially lost it and it showed. Mustering my last shred of human decency, I gathered my manners and stood up to meet her eyes with mine.

"I'm sorry," my tone was a mix of sharp and resigned, "I don't mean to be rude and I really *am* a good mom. We've just been traveling from California to New York and it's been a nightmare of a trip: The kids hate their car seats, I think my husband hates me. No one's pooping. No one's sleeping..."

I'm giving her all my personal information as she's staring at me, probably afraid I'm going to give her the "how often we've had sex" report (don't ask.) And I went on to introduce the fun-filled cast,

"See, there's my husband, Rock," I pointed to the door where he was carrying the baby in his arms, "and I'm basically just lucky he hasn't killed me yet."

I looked at this stranger, after delivering my depressing monologue. It was eerily quiet between us and she looked as if she'd seen a ghost.

"*What's. Your. Name?*" She whispered dramatically.

"Stacey Robbins?" I answered hesitantly, not sure after all those days on the road with my kids.

The woman paused and stage-whispered slowly and incredulously:

"*STACEY!*

It's *ME!*

NANCY!

FROM *ALASKA!!!*"

I'm thinking, *What is she talking about? I've never even been to Alaska.*

Her eyes were wide with anticipation of me connecting the dots.

Nancy... Nancy... Nancy from Alaska... who is this person? I was wracking my McDonald's filled, sleep-deprived brain.

When it finally hit me.

A year before our trip, my friend Julie had given me a spiritual guidance book. In the back, there's a phone number to call this organization affiliated with the book, in case you want someone to talk to as you walk through the chapters and the spiritual process.

I was confused by the third page of chapter one and called -- and was promptly assigned a counselor. I talked to her almost every week up until a few weeks before our big move to New York. Never met her. Didn't even know what she looked like.

That counselor's name was Nancy.

She was from Anchorage, Alaska.

And was now standing across from me

In a town, I hadn't planned on stopping in
In a hotel I hadn't planned on staying in
In a lobby breakfast bar, I hadn't planned on eating in

Nancy, from Alaska.

Who happened to be in town for a last minute conference in Harrisburg, Pennsylvania,
At the exact moment I hadn't planned on being here.

Uh-mazing.

She pointed to me -- this spiritual guide in my life -- and said,

"Do you know how much God loves you and me, to do this for us?"

I just smiled at her enthusiasm and hugged her.

Every wrong turn
Every delayed moment
Every frustrating stop

On our freaking ridiculous road trip from hell...

These were part of the answers to my big, desperate question of "*Why, God, why??*"

Assuring me that not everything that happens is just to frustrate me
Sometimes it's to surprise me, awaken me
And remind me.

That life isn't always what I see
And that sometimes, those hard times that seem more like obstacles
Are actually orange cones, redirecting me
And leading me to some unexpected "Holy crow, are you kidding me??" kind of goodness.

The kind that's more than I could even imagine
And more than I could ever dream.

20
The Mountain, The Mirror, and Me

"I feel like such a failure, Ken. I've totally blown it..."

He could hear the defeat in my voice from 3,000 miles away, even with the scratchy cell phone connection from the middle-of-nowhere town I had moved to in Upstate New York.

It was my best friend, Ken, in California, who was the big brother I had always wanted and finally had. Sharing an Italian heritage, a distinct passion for talking with our hands, and sporting, what is lovingly referred to as a "strong nose," people often asked if he and I were related. I could see why and it was more than the looks; we were both intensely, well... *intense* people.

Ken was five years older than me and at least 10 times more like a dog with a bone than I was. I called myself an A-type personality (when I was younger and my adrenal glands were working).

Ken called himself a "Triple A" personality and I think he underestimated by at least an A or two...

Or maybe six.

I knew of Ken before we ever actually became friends.

I had heard him on the radio when I was in a bit of a funk. I was sitting in my car one afternoon, after visiting my dad in the hospital, I had to take a moment to pause and transition out of the "Oh my god, my dad is dying" into "I have to teach my piano students" mode. Real life just keeps going, even when you want to make time stop.

I clicked the tuner to some station and landed, mid-story, to some super expressive guy telling a wild account of something that had happened in his life. I sat riveted by the voice of this strong man with an incredulous story and thought, "God, what a cool guy -- I'd love to meet him. I'd love to be his friend."

I turned off the radio, got out of my car and promptly forgot that I had said that.

A few months after my dad had passed, we moved out of our apartment on the west side and we found ourselves a nice two-story townhouse on the east side of town. A few months later, the townhouse next to us became available and yup, that's when Mr. Radio Story Guy ended up moving next door to me -- and I mean right next door -- where his townhouse and ours shared the very same wall.

Our families came to know and love each other; his kids were little littles, while we had none at the time.

While Ken and I were in the red zones of any Type-A chart you could put us in, his wife, Lynette and my husband, Rock, shared similar personalities: easy-going, laid-back, quick to flash a great smile and sporting a supernatural gift of being able to let the little things, and often the big things, go.

Ken and I would sit on my white, shabby-chic couch, sipping red wine as we covered everything from politics to conspiracy theories to eschatology. You know, stuff about death and hell and God's judgment -- all the makings of a spiritual horror movie in one conversation and a bottle of wine. Meanwhile Rock and Lynette would be laughing on the patio all relaxed and good-natured talking about the pleasant things in life and would occasionally come over to fill our glasses and remind us to lighten up.

I probably need to let you know this, too: you could be fooled by Ken's long hair, faded blue jeans, flip flops, and musician status and think "Oh, that dude's such a hippie" at first glance, but the minute he locked his relentless gaze to yours and opened his mouth, you knew that he was one of those brilliant, rock-star brainiacs. One of those guys who wrote and produced music that was smart enough to end up on KISS albums and award-winning epic movies. He was someone who was trusted by both the children on his son's soccer teams to lead them to victory and trusted by the President of the United States to be present at the signing of Sudan Peace Act for all of Ken's work to help those in South Sudan (true story). He's leapt out of his car in heroic ways (but never thinking he was heroic) to help a friend, a stranger -- or even an enemy in need (another true story).

But Ken was someone you definitely didn't want to enter into the dark alley of mindless conversation with. He would eat you for breakfast, lunch, and dinner and make you wish you had stayed home with your brioche, weak coffee, and blind presumptions rather than venturing out into his world of well-thought out considerations.

He didn't suffer fools lightly.

But when he loved you, it was a balls-to-the-wall
100%
All-in
Until Death Do Us Part
Kind of way he did everything else in life.

Triple A Personality-Type
Love.

His circle of influence was huge but his circle of trusted companions was small.

I was in that small, trusted circle and deeply honored to be there.

I loved being his friend,
But I loved even more that he was mine.

So, there I was 10 years later into our friendship, having moved from being his next door neighbor to him being the godfather of my children. Now Rock, the boys and I were on our 2-year job assignment on the East Coast amd Ken and I were on the hit-or-miss reception phone call where I was regaling him with one story after another about "her." "Her" being the woman who hired me for the East Coast assignment. The one who I left the comfort and flip-flops of Southern California for snow-covered everything in Upstate New York...the one who was a mix of The Devil Wears Prada and my mother. Slightly button-pushing, to say the least. It was the place where I thought I was going to do my work but the whole experience left me teetering on the edge of an identity crisis.

This wasn't the first time it had ever happened, by the way, that "teetering-on-the-edge-of-my-identity" thing.

But this time was different

(like "these times" usually are).

Because I had thought I was so much more enlightened after all the other "'these times." I thought for sure that I wasn't going to end up as a student stuck in the detention hall of this lesson...

Again.

The one with the passive/aggressive female who had a love/hate relationship with me -- loved me at first with all of my promise, talents, and charisma, and had judged me to be special -- but then, she saw the other parts of me: the "all" of me, which included my insecurities and inconsistencies And humanity.

For which I received a serious dose of rejection and blame, followed by me, trying to leap over the Grand Canyon of her disappointment, as if I could perform my way across the chasm of her unrealistic,

idealistic estimation of me.
Which I couldn't
So, I failed.

I failed her
And I failed me.

Again.

"She is such a bitch, Stacey," said my uber cut-to-the-chase friend, Ken. "And she's been such a bitch since you got there. Why don't you just pack up and come home?"

Never one to mince words, Ken's question bristled me to my core, as his questions usually did, because it touched that place in me that heard these unspoken thoughts,

And why do you keep getting yourself into situations where someone makes it hard for you to succeed? Why do you keep setting yourself up to try to please someone who is so essentially displeased by you?

In other words,

Why do you let someone treat you this way?

But instead of addressing the root of the problem, I spoke to the symptoms:

"Ken, I've blown it -- I know that I have. She seems so disappointed that I'm not who she thought I was...and now I'm not what she wanted. And if I can just figure out how to make it right, then I want to do that. I'd rather leave here a success than a failure. I just need more time to figure this out." My hollow protestations vaporized like smoke rings into the thick, dark, silence.

Ken isn't one to roll his eyes. Nope. He'll take his already laser-type gaze and focus it even more in those moments when excuses don't withstand the litmus test of reality. I could feel his eyes burning a hole in me from 3,000 miles away.

"Stacey…" his voice quickly shifted to that soft kindness he saves only for family, "She's not please-able. It's an illusion."

Just as quickly, his tone changed back to fierce protection, "For someone to take so much specific effort to focus on your imperfections, when you have so much good in you, says something about *her*. She doesn't want you to win, she wants to be right about you so, she's not going to let you win. Knowing that, why would you even try?"

Apparently the question was rhetorical because he kept going, "All she's focusing on is what you are not, Stacey." His voice softened again, "Honey, you are so much more than what you are not. You are not the sum total of your weaknesses."

My shoulders sank with relief. It's amazing how truth can make you breathe. I exhaled so hard releasing those toxic lies I had been holding onto that it made me want to sob,

Or laugh.

Actually, both.

I am so much more than I am not. I am not the sum total of my weaknesses.

That's when I knew the bigger truth: That how I was feeling and where I was at with "this bitch" had nothing to do with her at all,

And everything to do with me.

Because it wasn't about how hard it was for me to please her, or how much harder I needed to work to find another way into her heart.

It was about how hard it was for me
To please that constantly critical, nagging, perfectionistic bitch
Inside of *me*.

———————

He told me it would happen

And he was right.

Jon Uhler had sat across from me in 1994 -- two years before I had met Ken and twelve years before I took that job in New York.

Jon was my counselor: a tall drink of water with dark hair, glasses, and a distracting Adam's apple bobbing up and down in a hypnotic way. It likely wouldn't have done that if he had 30 more pounds on his long frame but it kind of added to the calming aspect of the therapeutic experience. He seemed more an artist and mystic trapped in a Psychology degree.

He was an enigma, for sure.

And I was his nightmare who showed up weekly with some *saga du jour* that left him incredulous at how someone who was 24 years old could have gone through -- and still be going through -- so much upheaval in her life. He listened just as passionately as he shared, not hiding behind some pious, aloof facade that many in his profession often do.

Nope.

Jon was right there with me -- being present to whatever I brought to the table. He was wide-eyed and entertained or tight-lipped and frustrated -- even flushing with anger up his long neck and cheeks depending on what story I was unfolding. He genuinely cared about me and I knew it. His love was a safe place.

So, in the space of being so intently heard and understood, I was able to hear him as he shared his life theories with me about

People
And mountains
And gifts.

"Stacey, you're going to find people in life who have different faces and different names, at different times and different places -- but they bring the same button-pushing qualities to you. That person who's being rejecting of you may leave your life, but do you notice how another rejecting person shows up soon after the other one leaves?

It would be easy to think it's about the other people but I want to tell you something: those people are a mountain -- a mountain that you're going to try to get around or sneak away from or travel in darkness so that you don't have to face it in full light, but God wants something more for you. He wants you to be unafraid of these people -- or anyone -- or any *thing* for that matter -- he wants to show you how you can get over that "mountain" with his help.

You see, Stacey..."

Jon leaned forward, resting his lanky arms on his knees and peering at me through his retro eyeglasses and said, "The person who's irritating you is a mountain and the mountain is a gift."

His words have lingered for years and while his words stayed with me, the depth of what he spoke more than two decades ago didn't fully reveal itself to me for a long while.

It takes some time
And perspective
To see people as mountains

And mountains as gifts.

Because it's tempting to be distracted by the person who's in front of you.

It's tempting to think it's about them and what they're doing to you instead of taking yourself one step away from the person and into the deeper question:

"Have I encountered the mountain of this personality before in my life?"

And in asking that, to get enough distance to stop focusing on the face of the individual and start asking yourself, "What have I done in the face of that mountain..."

When that person was rejecting
Or judgmental
Or doubtful of my abilities
Or condescending with my opinions
Or defensive to my questions
Or angry with my honesty
Or betraying of my vulnerability
Or abusive with my trust
Or challenging to my integrity
Or mocking of my faith
Or undermining of my efforts

And on and on.

The question eventually stops being about how to stop the other person from being that way and becomes a broader question, "How do I live in the face of non-agreement and opposition wherever it shows up in life...

No matter what name or face it has?"

Eventually, and thankfully, even that question can transform into something so sharp and specific that it actually burns, "How do I live with the part of me that isn't in agreement with my true divine value? How do I live with the part of me that's in opposition to my dreams?"

I didn't realize for many years that I was my own enemy. In fact, it really didn't hit me until I was diagnosed with an autoimmune dis-ease.

An autoimmune dis-ease is when your body starts attacking itself. It sees itself as a foreign object -- an enemy, rather than a friend -- and it sends out all of these antibodies to fight against it.

In essence, it's at war with itself.

For years I wondered, "How did I get this?" And eventually I asked myself, "How could I not have gotten this?"

The pattern became so clear.

Being the child -- the child scared, in a house that looked great on the outside but was fighting against itself on the inside.

A household where truth was malleable and moody -- and if you didn't adjust your truth to match the constantly moving target of constantly-changing truth, it meant that you were disloyal.

So, if someone said the sky was purple and you said you saw blue, that was disloyal.

And if you were disloyal by representing your truth, love got taken away
Advocacy was gone
Protection disappeared
And punishment prevailed.

As a child, I felt my truth in my gut and in my chest and a lot of times, I felt it in my throat.
I attempted to make the pain go away through food, or physical relationships, or alcohol.

I kept trying to find ways to deal with the pain of being "me" in an atmosphere that wasn't allowing it. I kept getting the message, "I love you and accept you, Stacey -- as long as you're nothing like you."

And then, one day, I just stopped feeling.

It cost too much to know the truth and to speak it to my family. It cost me love.

So, I divorced my body and all of its instincts and intuitions and climbed up into my head.

As a child, I lived up there in my imaginations and fantasy world -- a voracious reader, hiding in a world where other people were allowed to feel and follow their intuitions and speak their truths.

I lived through them since I wasn't living through me.

And when, I got older, I stopped reading and started thinking.

Overthinking, actually.

Imagining in a different way -- a negative way: Wondering what people thought when I said this thing or that thing that quieted them. Wondering what people thought of me in those clothes, or at that weight. Wondering what people thought of me singing that song and marrying that man.

My brain was in constant motion, relentlessly twisting and turning the mental Rubix cube trying to make the colors of my life match up. Trying to figure out the cues of when people were pleased or displeased with me and trying to anticipate their needs so that I could meet them.

So that they wouldn't be disappointed.

So that I wouldn't lose their love.

I stayed in my head for the longest time, losing the sense of my body except to punish it for getting tired or for gaining weight when I wanted it to stay thin and sexy. I'd beat it up with ridiculous diets, long hours at work, and too little sleep.

I did that for years until it waved its little white flag.

It couldn't take it anymore and I got sick
And had to pay attention to it.

This body.

Oh how I resented it for failing me -- for running out of steam.

I eventually asked the question, "How do I get better?"

The answer that came was, *Take care of your Self. Take care of your body. Listen to it. It's trying to tell you something.*

How do you listen to something that you had stopped paying attention to? How do you get it to talk to you, when it had to resort to screaming because it's been ignored by the "you" it's living within?

How do you assure your Self, "I won't be mad if you need to rest. I won't be frustrated if you need to go slowly and take your time. I won't betray you and overwork you the second you start healing. I won't demand you to be different than you are."

I didn't know how to do that with myself.

No one had taught me.

For a while I lingered in the victimhood of that thought: the *No one taught me and somebody else did this to me* thought.

But that thinking only works if you're committed to seeing your Self as disabled so that you can qualify for emotional welfare.

That thinking doesn't work if you want to be well and strong and to help others be well and strong, too.

So, I had to let go of being the victim and all the unbeneficial kind of benefits that came with that -- and I stepped out into a question to the Source of me and asked,

"How do I love my Self?"

And it was there, in that question I was willing to take back my power to love *me* -- that the journey took off in a healing direction.

Every time I encountered someone who wasn't loving me, it was so tempting to retreat back into my head and try to figure out what I had done wrong.

Like with that woman in New York.

Or those many other people who came before her
Or have come since.

But it's not about them.

It's about me being on the journey of discovering all over, again (and in some ways for the first time) how to love my Self.

When that happens, that person across from you stops being a

mountain
And they start being a mirror.

The face is my own
The mountain is me
And seeing it for what it is
Is the gift of finally being able to journey

Back to Truth
To Love
To Freedom
To Passion
To Self-Expression

To Health.

The journey over the mountain
Is the journey
To the Source and Creator
To Spirit.

The journey over that mountain of how I've been in my own way
With the thoughts and beliefs that didn't serve me
But they served my weak thoughts and strong stories.

Every person I encounter
Who looks like a mountain
Leads me back home

To *me.*

21
Walking Differently in the Same Direction

I love the beach.

Living in Southern California makes a lot of sense to my soul after growing up as a Jersey girl who spent her summers at "the shore." The ocean and I are friends. In fact, I tell my husband,

"It helps me breathe."

He looks at me with a funny smile, "How can water help you breathe?"

"I don't know. Maybe my spirit animal and my astrological sign have hooked up under water... all I know is that if I go to Vegas for three days, I feel like I've been buried alive in the desert."

"Most people feel like that after visiting Vegas for three days." He rubbed his fingers and thumb together -- the universal symbol for "losing money in Las Vegas" - *like you know we have.*

"No silly, you know what I mean... as soon as we drive back and I see the ocean, it's like oxygen to me."

He tilted his head to the left -- maybe hoping I'd make more sense from a different angle, "You know, you barely go *in* the ocean."

Ummm, yeah.

He's right.

The movie Jaws pretty much killed that for me -- and a scrillion other

American kids in the mid-1970's. (Did I mention that when I went running from the dark theatre, mid-movie with my heart and head pounding in terror -- that the bathroom walls were painted blood red? Yeah. Pretty much sealed the deal.)

So despite my wild fear of walking into the water and, at best, stepping on something slimy that wiggles under my feet -- or at worst, encountering a Great White Shark,

I can confidently say this:

The ocean calls to me.

With that said, there's this weird thing, though, that I've noticed since we moved to a new location a little further north along the coast: the last few times when I was out for a walk, I had to remind myself to look at the water.

The boardwalk (which is actually concrete and not made of boards where we live) is a little different than I'm used to. There are no beachfront homes and charming stores that flank the path. Instead, on the left, you hear the sounds of the cars and motorcycles zooming by on Pacific Coast Highway (PCH). Straight ahead, you see more flat boardwalk, and the spit from phlegm-y joggers who went running by.

Super ick.

And, to the right, because the boardwalk is a little lower than the sand, you only see sand and sky. You know the ocean's there but you just can't see it from where you are.

I feel disoriented here.

And then, as we walk a little further, the ground levels up and my husband will say, "There's the ocean!" as if it had been hiding on us.

I've literally had to turn my head to a strong 45 degree right angle and been surprised, in a "Oh yes, you're right! Now, look at that." kind of way. Because, despite the obvious atmosphere, I could walk right there and completely miss it.

Rock turned to me a few days ago on our morning jaunt and said, "You know, we can walk on the *actual* sand. We're allowed to do that, you know."

I looked at him as if he were speaking Chinese. It was winter here and despite the fact that it's NOTHING like the winters I had growing up in New Jersey and Connecticut, I will say this:

I was freezing.

No snow. No ice. Just air that's so close to the water, that it feels like it's slicing through my bones. Visitors wear shorts and flips while I'm sporting two tops, a sweater, scarf and a hat. *And pants. I figured you assumed that, but it's Southern California and all bets for presuming people would wear pants here are pretty much off.*

It's not just the air that's cold: The sand is cold, too.

After nearly 30 years of ~~torturing~~ being married to my husband, he knows that my brain short-circuits so, he stated the obvious: "You can keep your shoes on AND walk on the sand."

And there we went: sashaying to the right, maybe 30-40 feet.

Within that teeny-tiny walk, it was as if some movie director suddenly called "Action!": The ocean roared. The sea air smelled salty. Surfers ran with their boards while seagulls flew overhead -- and those little weird, hop-on-one-leg birds were using their tweezer-like bills to pull crabs from the sand as the waves rolled back.

Life, miraculously, came to life.

It was there the whole time, but I couldn't see it until I shifted.

Thirty feet to the right, I was walking in the same direction, but in a completely different world.

———————

A lot of my life has been about learning how to shift.

That happens when things don't go exactly as you have planned -- and I've had a lot of... well, let's just say, *opportunities*, to practice.

Whether it's the unexpected move to a new town when you're a kid Or an unexpected health issue as an adult

Or just pretty much anything in between.

Life changes, and if we don't adjust with it, it just makes it harder on *us*.

I remember when my husband and I went to a spa and did a challenge course -- *even though I definitely think spas are more for massages than climbing telephone poles and jumping off -- alas, we climbed telephone poles and jumped off.*

When my husband, who went first (because they said, "If you normally go last, go first" so, up he went) got all the way to the top, he was about to stand up tall and have a proud James Cameron "King of the World!" moment when, suddenly he panicked, bent his knees and almost fell. Because, just as he was about to celebrate the climb, the round disk platform, barely large enough to hold his size 15 feet, swiveled.

The leader of the experience reminded us that sometimes, when you think you're done, and you've arrived, life changes.

And boy howdy, does it.

I remember how I felt when I found out, not long after we were married, that my husband was struggling with some compulsive behaviors. They had started in his teen years but he didn't tell me when we got married when I was 20. When I found out about a year later, I was pissed, hurt, and felt so lied to and rejected.

I thought marriage meant you were both on the same page and moving forward.

It doesn't always mean that. I found that out, the uncomfortable way.

I tried to stay there for a long time -- in the hurt, resentful place.

I kept looking at him, like he had set himself on fire, waiting for the fire to go out, telling him 27,000 times a day *how* and *why* he should be putting the fire out. Meanwhile, 6 years went by while he was still in flames, yet I was the one consumed.

Finally, I said to myself: *That's it. I'm not waiting anymore. I have my own stuff to work on. I'm committed to our marriage but I can't focus on what he has to work on.*

And you know what happened in that seventh year?

He got free of that thing that had been tormenting him since he was a teen.

Not only did shifting my expectations change something for me, I truly believe that it gave a wider space for things to change for him.

I coach women who've gone through worse.

I have sat with brilliant, beautiful, dedicated souls who've invested their whole life and early adult years devoted to their husbands, only to be left for a younger woman.

The resentment is s-t-r-o-n-g, as you can imagine and understand. I hear things like, "Wait! I already worked so hard. I don't want to start over!! I gave my best years to him! This is *not* fair."

And they're right. It's super suck-y and not fair.

And if they stay in that place and never shift out of staring at their feet and start walking again, they will never really live the life they're here to live.

So the energy spent on long-term resentment or wishing it were different, is really needed elsewhere: It's needed to shift.

Usually the biggest hurdle is our expectation from "The way I thought it would be" to "This is the way it is."

It's not always so easy -- no matter who you are -- I've seen 116 pound women and 225 pound weight-lifters not be able to get out of a stuck position, despite how light or strong they are.

Because it's not about your strength or lightness -- it's about your beliefs. The mind game matters. Like Henry Ford said, "Whether you think you can or you think you can't, you're right."

I think the mind gets set in place when we're young, during those early developmental years. We get trained to think we can't reach for this goal, or accomplish that dream. We get stuck in a story of doubt and unbelief about ourselves and believe that life is bigger than us, instead of believing we're big enough for life. And then, when we grow up and have the power of freedom and capacity to do something more, we don't use either because we don't believe we can.

I remember reading about how baby elephants are trained by being shackled with heavy chains to a tree. When they try to take a step, the chains around their legs stop them. Eventually they get the message, "You're not strong enough for that" so, that when they're older and massive, with the strength that can crush almost anything in their path, they are only held to a tree by a light rope.

They don't even bother trying to get away, because they don't believe they can.

We relish the children's story of *The Little Engine that Could* because we get excited to see a more empowering mindset prevail.

So, shifting. How do we do it? Those beliefs that have us locked up in chains. How do we break them and believe that we can?

———————

In 1995, I went to a weekend experience. My marriage was in a weird place (my husband was still on fire at the time, and I was still watching him burn) my relationship with my divorced parents was in a weird place, and I kept running into the same walls in life, trying to figure out why the walls were chasing me.

At that weekend, they talked more about stories -- the stories we believe, as if they're true and then, react to, as if they're true.

It was just a massive revelation for me, to consider that they weren't true.

That my mother being mad at me didn't mean I was an awful person. That my father raising a hand to me, didn't mean I was unworthy of being protected -- that my husband having his on-fire issues didn't mean that I was undeserving of love.

That was profound for me.

I had sat for so many years, just assuming that my conclusions were true.
To be able to question them and become the curious observer instead of the reactor was a huge shift for me.
It changed my entire life.

One day, I woke up and my tongue was orange.

Not just any kind of orange -- it was like someone had taken a Crayola, Burnt Sienna crayon, ripped the paper off and rubbed the side of it all over my tongue, kind of orange.

Oh my lord, what is happening to me?

It was in the middle of all of my crazy, dizzy symptoms and feeling awful in my health. And now, I had a freakin' orange, alien tongue.

Perfect.

I showed my tongue to everyone. My husband, my neighbor across the street who's a nurse, her nextdoor neighbor who's kids babysat my kids --

And then, I drove across town to my doctor's office.

"Can you thee this? My thongue is oranthe!"

Yes, they saw.

And a scrillion doctors and expensive tests later, nobody knew what was wrong with my tongue or me.

I was so discouraged. I prayed daily for wisdom, did research on the internet, invested what was left of our money to try to figure out what was wrong with my body. Months and months went by -- still dizzy, still an orange tongue.

Still no answers.
I sat in the tub, with my scrunched-up forehead one afternoon, "God, I've been asking for wisdom for so long on this. Can you please just give me wisdom?"

I blew the air of frustration from between my lips, feeling defeated and alone, when Words with No Voice sent this,

"Your wisdom is in the unknown."

Huh?

My brain was saying *"That doesn't even make sense."*

But my spirit was saying,

"Yes."

I started repeating to myself:

Your wisdom is in the unknown...
Your wisdom is in the unknown...

It started to open up to me -- the idea that what I don't know, could actually be some kind of gift -- and maybe there was a wisdom hiding there.

I settled into the tub a little deeper -- into this sacred moment -- willing to embrace the unknown instead of wishing it away.

And as I did that, I had this deep, deep sense that an answer was coming soon. A few days later, my generous girlfriend, Cathy, called and offered the boys and me tickets to Disneyland. Living 20 minutes away from the theme park makes that part easy, but dealing with dizziness and children, rides and crowds, makes it not.

"Dizzyland" didn't sound like a whole lotta fun to this momma.

But I felt guilty -- the kids have been stuck in the house and the yard with me through so much of this. I know I could send them alone with my husband, but I want to share some fun experiences with them and not just the hard ones. So, I said, "Yes, thank you."
And off we went.

I walked slowly while Rock and the boys rushed ahead. They jumped onto Thunder Mountain, while I found a bench in the shade and checked on my phone.

There was an Asian woman next to me and boy, was she chatty. I kept "Mmmhmmm"-ing her and looking more closely at my phone, hoping she'd take a hint.

She didn't.

I was feeling exasperated when I heard these words inside of me,

Sometimes, when someone won't stop talking, it's because they have a gift to give you.

Okay, fine. I closed my phone and turned my attention to her with a forced little smile on my face.

"So tell me about you…"

Which she did. She was from a very busy city in China and had been out in the US for 10 years. San Diego, to be more precise, and was up for a few days with her kids and grandkids to enjoy the wonders of Orange County. I nodded and asked, "Was it stressful in the city where you're from in China?"

She was emphatic, "Yes. Very."

I asked, "Did people have a lot of thyroid problems there?"
My journey with health was in a "All roads lead to thyroid questions" kind of phase.

She looked surprised, "Well, yes, actually. We have a high rate of thyroid issues there. And I know that because I was a medical doctor in China."

I was stunned. She went on to share about how, when she came over to the US, her degrees weren't accepted here and she went on to become a master herbalist instead, which was her current profession in San Diego.

"Can I ask you a question?" I asked her.

"Yes." she answered, probably hearing that a lot.

So, I stuck my tongue out at her.

After I put it back in my mouth, I asked, "Do you know why my tongue is orange?"

She smiled, "Oh yes. That's easy. That's a deficiency in the blood. You take lots of vitamin D, eat green apples, meats and vegetables, and walk 2 ½ hours a day and it will go away."

I looked at her, incredulous.

What no one else could figure out or help me make go away, she was saying was easy. I thanked her for the guidance, and the Divine for the wisdom -- despite my best efforts to shut it out because it wasn't showing up in conventional ways.

I did what she said and four days later, the orange on my tongue disappeared.

Something happened in the tub that day. I saw the same circumstances of not having answers, differently and then ended up with a different experience. Even though I don't completely understand what happened.

I can't deny that it did.

―――――――――

Sometimes I stay in my head -- in thinking mode about stuff -- and I expect things to change.

I can think about eating right all day long (while I devour a pan of brownies) and it's not going to get me to my goal.

I can think about the dream relationships, but if I never leave the house and say "Hello" to someone, how am I going to connect?

I can think about going on my dream trip to Italy, but if I never make a plan, buy the tickets, and get on the plane, I'm never going to get there.

That doesn't mean that thinking and dreaming and working on things in your brain isn't valuable -- because it is. I'm just talking about the times when all we do is stay in our head. There's a reason that the phrase is "Lights! Camera! Action!" - it's because if we were all "Lights!" and "Camera!" there'd be nothing to see.

We need the "Action!"

Tony Robbins shares that if he's feeling a little out of sorts, he plunges himself into freezing water because the physical action shifts the direction his mind is going.

We know that in yoga, doing the poses can actually restore parts of the brain and help to heal PTSD.

Taking actions can shift us in different directions.

I know it sounds so simple and basic, but I had this wild revelation one day while waiting on line to talk to a speaker at an event. I heard this inner voice say to me, "You're waiting for things to be just right. You're waiting for your feelings to feel just right. Don't wait. Start now. As imperfect as it might be, just do something, now."

I'm pretty brave in a lot of places but in some ways, I get stuck.

I was still waiting for Monday to start the perfect diet.
Or the financial windfall to make my dreams come true.

As enlightened as I can be, some parts of me are still sucking my thumb.

Sometimes, it's not thinking through the thing one more time -- sometimes it's just getting up off your duff and doing something.

So, I started adding that as a mantra in my life: "Don't wait, start." And amazing things happened: I started new businesses, books, and traveled all over.

One of my all-time favorite shifting actions, is something 100-Day Gong.

It's not the big, bronze thing you hit with a mallet. Nope practice where you do the same thing, every day, straight. Whether it's yoga or meditating, or writir book-writing or pole dancing or whatever -- you can make up what your good-for-you thing is, and do it for 100 Days straight. If you miss a day, you start over - even if you're on Day 99.

It's radically changed my life since I started doing it in 2014 because it can radically alter your brain through the process.

We know that the brain builds and breaks lifelong habits at around the 90 day mark. To do 100 days is like running past the finish line, like your track and field coach taught you to do. And those hundred days are pure gold.

Because it helps you see how you handle life: In the beginning when it's exciting, in the middle when it's dark and messy, when you're near the end and you're tempted to sabotage your success.

And all those places in between when you feel out of sorts, or someone pisses you off, or you have to take a trip, or something.

You know, all those Life-somethings that happen all the time and we let them get in our way.

The Gong helps you see what's going on in your head -- your story, your chains -- and your commitment to keep going, proves to you that the stories are lies.

It's so freakin' powerful.

Who knew by doing yoga and meditation every day for 100 days, that the naggy, bitchy voice in my head would go away and be replaced by a kinder, gentler voice that cheered me on?

that my sleep would improve?
hat my moods would even out?
at my outlook on life would be more optimistic?

Sometimes we never know what is possible until we take an action -- in the face of our feelings and stories -- and then we are able to see the power that comes just by doing a little bit, consistently, over a long period of time.

Shifting happens in many ways and in many places.

While you or I may not do the more extreme things of jumping into freezing waters like Tony Robbins does or out of perfectly good airplanes like some of my friends do, we can still make great changes in our relationships, our jobs and our way of interacting with life.
My favorites are yoga, meditation, going on a traveling adventure, gratitude, listening to a podcast, making love, watching something funny, reading something profound, taking a class...

Just moving a little bit in a different direction, takes us from:

Feeling defeated to feeling empowered
From the bitchy voice to the encouraging one
from the spit on the sidewalk to the front of the ocean.

Like my wonderful friend and writer, Tracy Panzarella says, "Shift right, shift left, just keep on shifting until you see the gift."

She knows what shifting's about -- living with a daughter with epilepsy means that Tracy has had to learn how to flex and flow and find new ways. She hasn't had the luxury of getting stuck in static thinking. She's an expert on shifting until she sees the gift.

That's the power that's inside all of us -- to notice what isn't working in our lives and to become the curious observer and the action taker; inviting the Divine to guide us with the wisdom that's available to each and every one of us, at all times.

Does it always work out smoothly or the way we want? Nope. I can definitely say that.

But I can say it makes a difference. Sometimes the shift happens in my circumstances. Sometimes it happens in my perspective and sometimes both.

What I do know is that it can make for better living, deeper loving, and more alive-ness to our experiences --

And *that* brings a lot of magic to the messy and mundane parts

Of this unconventional life.

Would love to stay connected at:

www.staceyrobbins.com